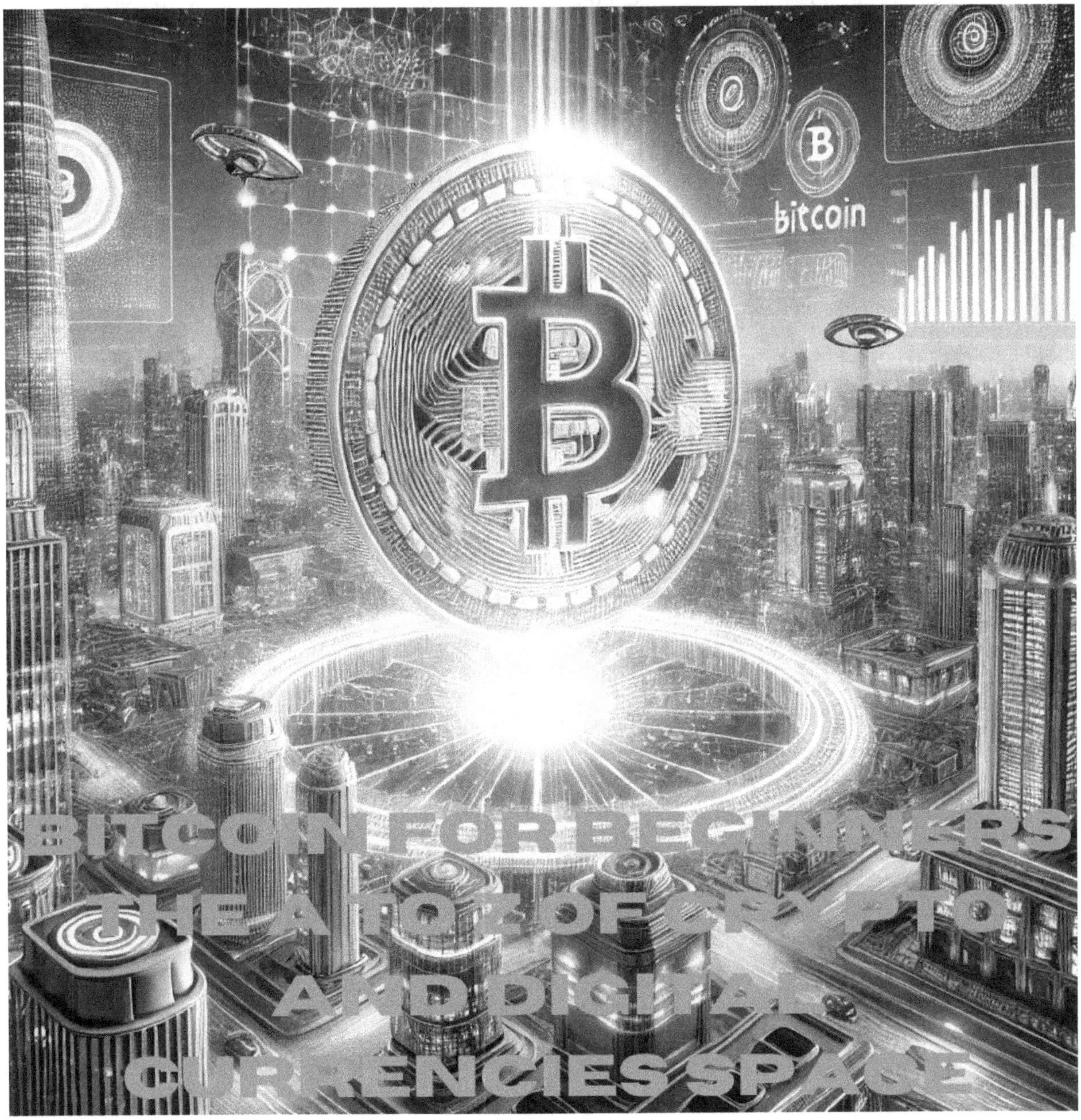
bitcoin
BITCOIN FOR BEGINNERS
THE A TO Z OF CRYPTO
AND DIGITAL
CURRENCIES SPACE

Introduction:

The question to be asked would be: What is Bitcoin?

In short,

Bitcoin is a sort of "free virtual currency", and, a decentralized asset. It is also called a cryptocurrency and is under control through blockchain technology. Mostly, Bitcoin is used for digital transactions, transferring values, and also works as a medium of exchange.

What does it mean?

"Free virtual currency" means it is not under control of one authority, for example, banks. In the normal or contemporary world system, your money is controlled through the banking sector. To this effect, no single transaction is allowed without your bank keeping track. It can also accept or discard any transaction. But not Bitcoin which is a completely free from any authority.

"Decentralized" means it's distributed to thousands of computers spread all over the world, impervious to all forms of censorship or manipulation.

"Cryptocurrencies"

Cryptocurrencies are digital or virtual currencies that make use of cryptography for security. Unlike traditional currencies, which are issued by governments, such as the US dollar or the euro, cryptocurrencies work on decentralized networks based on blockchain technology, a distributed ledger enforced by a network of computers called nodes.

"Blockchain technology"

Most modern cryptocurrencies base their applications on blockchain technologies. In simple words, blockchain can be imagined to be some sort of a component public ledger on which each and every transaction with a certain cryptocurrency is recorded. With regard to these wallets, this provides for all attributes of transparency, hence security and being immutable; in this sense, blockchain transactions cannot be modified once recorded.

The aim of this book, in other words, is that through it, an answer to every question that may come into one's mind in regard to this new technology and its future will be answered in the simplest way in order to be understood by anyone.

For this purpose, we have gathered 59 most asked questions for you to be able to know everything you need to know about this revolutionary and futuristic technology.

This book is addressed for anyone who has heard about Bitcoin and cryptocurrencies, who want to know more and understand this new technology. A step-by-step guide, so that nothing remains unexplained or unanswered.

Let us start from the beginning and ask questions in order.

1- What is Crypto? What is Bitcoin?

2- What is Ethereum?

3- Why was crypto invented?

4 - When was it invented?

5- Who invented Bitcoin? what is bitcoin white paper?

6- What was it invented for?

7- How cryptos are created? What is mining, minting?

8- Mining of Bitcoin and minting of Cryptos.

9- How to mine Bitcoin?

10- What is blockchain?

11- which came first, Bitcoin or blockchain?

12- What is blockchain, and what benefits does it have within a business?

13- What are smart contracts?

14- What are Proof of Work (POW) and Proof of stake (POS)?

15- What is the minimum value of Bitcoin that I can purchase?

16- Adoption of Cryptos today.

17- Cryptos adoption since creation.

18- Will crypto replace money as we know it?

19- Who uses crypto today, and who will use it tomorrow?

20- Is Crypto available to all?

21- What is a Crypto exchange?

22- What is DeFi (Decentralized Finance)?

23- What is a cryptocurrency wallet?

24- What is a crypto address?

25- Where and how to buy cryptos?

26- Where and how to store cryptos?

27 -Hot and cold cryptos storage.

28- Is it risky?

29- Can it be stolen?

30- What is a Bitcoin ETF?

31- How to send and receive cryptocurrencies?

32- What are Gas fees?

33- How many cryptos are at the market today?

34- What are the cryptos different types?

35- Difference between the crypto coins and types.

36- What are the different uses of cryptos?

37- Difference between crypto coins versus tokens

38- Buy crypto coins or crypto tokens?

39- What are stable coins?

40- Can I mix between different coins?

41- What are NFTs (Non fungible tokens)?

42- What are DApps?

43- Will crypto go to zero?

44- Can I spend crypto like cash?

45- Can I get a crypto debit or credit card?

46- Can I use cryptocurrencies worldwide?

47- Can I borrow money using cryptos?

48- Can I earn interest with crypto?. What is stacking?

49- Will governments adopt crypto?

50- Is it worldwide adopted?

51- Can it be duplicated?

52- Is cryptocurrency taxed?

53- Bitcoin or fiat? (Government printed money).

54- Safety of Bitcoin compared to Fiat (Normal printed money)

55- Bitcoin or gold?

56- Invest in Bitcoin or Gold?

57- Crypto adoption in the future.

58- Which countries are crypto friendly today?

59- Biggest owners of Bitcoin today

1.What is Crypto? What is Bitcoin?

Cryptocurrencies are digital or virtual currencies that actually employ cryptography to secure all the transactions. As opposed to traditional, government-issued currencies-such as the United States dollar or the euro for example-cryptocurrencies function through decentralized systems based on blockchain: a distributed ledger forced through a network of computers called nodes.

In other words:

1. Decentralization:
Most of the virtual currencies are decentralized; thus, they depend on a peer-to-peer network. They are not controlled by any kind of central authority such as government and financial corporation.

2. Blockchain Technology:
While most are at their very core based on blockchain, blockchain is a type of public ledger that keeps track of whatever kinds of transactions are involved with any given cryptocurrency. It confers properties of transparency, security, and immutability: once something is recorded, it can never be changed.

3. Cryptography:
Cryptocurrencies are the virtual money using cryptography for the security of transactions, controlling the creation of more units, and verification of asset transfer. Public and private keys form part of this use case in enabling people to securely send and receive cryptocurrency.

4. Digital and Virtual:
Cryptocurrencies are completely digital and don't exist in reality as coins or notes. They are kept in what is called digital wallets-software or hardware-based on computers, smartphones, or any other physical devices designed to keep digital assets secure.

5. Global with no boundaries:
They allow for almost instantaneous, borderless cash transfer and overall, are faster and cheaper ways of banking than more traditional methods. They can also be utilized by anyone with internet access.

6. Limitation of supply:
Whereas most of the cryptocurrencies are designed to be of limited supply, in most cases, this fact has usually been predetermined by their underlying code. Examples include Bitcoin, which has a capped supply of 21 million coins, adding to its scarcity and consequential value.

7. Volatility:
The prices are highly volatile, hence alteration within the shortest time can be high. That might be a point of profit or huge loss for the investors or traders.

Examples of some popular cryptocurrencies include:

- Bitcoin (BTC): First and most recognized cryptocurrency, which came into this world in 2009 by a person or group of people using the pseudonym Satoshi Nakamoto. It has become so used everywhere that the terminology "digital gold" has been used.

- Ethereum is a blockchain-based platform that was founded in 2015 with smart contract functionality deployed by developers who need it to build and deploy dApps. Ethereum hosts its own cryptocurrency, called Ether, required to be used to pay for transactions on its network.

- Ripple (XRP): While designed for fast and cheap cross-border settlement, Ripple nonetheless is a protocol of payment settlement and one particular cryptocurrency. It targets cross-border transactions between a variety of financial institutions.

- Litecoin (LTC): Litecoin was going to be a "lighter" version of Bitcoin. Conceived in 2011 by Charlie Lee, Litecoin boasts much faster transaction times and operates on a different hashing algorithm.

-Cardano is a blockchain platform similar to Ethereum, although in implementation, it relies on the latter for security and scaling. By design, it's a proof-of-stake consensus mechanism that finally targets a more viable and efficient blockchain.

Uses and Applications of Virtual Currencies:
Digital Payments: The cryptocurrencies can be utilized for buying something online, and also at some outlets physically, which thereby presents an alternative to conventional modes of paying for goods and services.

Investment: Individuals invest heavily in the purchase of cryptocurrencies, which they hope will appreciate in value over time. For this very reason and motive, a market for cryptocurrency came into existence where traders can buy and sell digital assets.

DeFi: short for Decentralized Finance, means the active use of cryptocurrencies in order to make real an important purpose: the recreation of traditional financial services around lending, borrowing, and trading through decentralized platforms.
This might imply from tokenization itself that tokens can manifest assets, rights, or access to some sort of services that might be traded or used within an ecosystem.

- Smart Contracts: Several other platforms, such as Ethereum, use the cryptocurrency underlying their respective blockchains in developing smart contracts. A smart contract is a self-executing contract that allows the agreement between two parties-or the contract terms-to be directly written into lines of code.

Counterpart: Difficulties and Dangers

Regulatory Uncertainty: Cryptocurrencies exhibit high variances in terms of legal status across countries. A change in regulations may drastically affect the value and usefulness of a cryptocurrency.

Security risks: While blockchain itself as an entity is highly secure, the broader ecosystem, like exchanges and wallets, is the more exposed point to the points of hacking and fraud.

High Volatility in the Market: This can further cause high volatility in cryptocurrencies and hence set up investors for great financial losses.

- Scalability: In as much as many new cryptocurrencies get to be popular, scalability has been the major headache for several of them. Facilities cannot scale to large users and transactions without losing speed and cost efficiency.

Cryptocurrencies opened completely new horizons: unsurpassed solutions and opportunities on one side, but very serious risks and challenges on the other.

2- What is Ethereum?

Ethereum is an open-source, decentralized, blockchain-based platform that enables users to build and deploy smart contracts and dApps. This was a proposal by the programmer Vitalik Buterin in late 2013 and was launched in 2015. Ethereum extends the basic blockchain concept brought in with Bitcoin by further allowing not just peer-to-peer payments but also complex, programmable applications.
It includes ETH, which is the native cryptocurrency utilized on the Ethereum chain to pay the transaction fee, computation services, and to execute smart contracts. Ethereum works on a decentralized set of computers that validate the blockchain and execute smart contracts in a way that is open, secure, and censorship-resistant.

The main ideas of Ethereum are:

- Smart Contract: A set of promises, in rule form encoded in lines of code that facilitates, verifies and enforces some sort of agreement or activity. Smart contracts also self-execute and are self-enforcing, meaning no intermediaries are needed.

- dApps: Shortened form for "Decentralized applications". These are applications on the Ethereum blockchain that run on a peer-to-peer network wherein no single party control it.

- EVM: The Ethereum Virtual Machine, the runtime environment for the execution of smart contracts on Ethereum that enables developers to execute codes in a decentralized way.

Ethereum has been the foundation for many innovations in the blockchain space, including the creation of decentralized finance (DeFi) platforms, non-fungible tokens (NFTs), and decentralized autonomous organizations (DAOs).

Ethereum is an open-source, decentralized blockchain platform that allows developers to create and deploy decentralized applications, including smart contracts. Ethereum was formally introduced in 2015, in a publication by Vitalik Buterin and a few others. Ethereum extends the usage of blockchain from mere cryptocurrency to programmable and complex applications and transactions with its native cryptocurrency called Ether, used to pay for the transaction fee and computational services.

3- Why was crypto invented?

Cryptocurrency was initiated to offer a decentralized type of digital currency which could work independently of conventional banking systems and out of the control of governments. Some of the important reasons underlying its development include:

Decentralized: Most of the cryptocurrencies, including Bitcoin, are made in a manner so that dependence on any middle authority-like banks or government bodies, which would rule over the passing of a transaction and eliminate every possible chance of corruption, censorship, or control of any authoritative power, would not be necessary.

Financial inclusion: it provides a way of giving basic financial services to people who do not have access to mainstream banking; it is particularly important for developing countries.

Lower Transaction Cost: Unlike conventional banking systems, which have been under massive criticism with growing transaction costs and slow processes in sending money across borders, digital cryptocurrencies reduce the transaction cost and speed up the process.

Security and Privacy: Most cryptos make use of specific cryptography to protect transactions from fraud. Most of them offer a degree of anonymity, hence great privacy for its transactions compared to conventional financial systems.

Anti-inflationary: The fact is very simple that some cryptocurrencies have their **fixed pre-supplied cap**, while each and every passing day more and more is printed of a particular fiat currency issued by the government.

These motivations brought together the first cryptocurrency, Bitcoin, crafted by an anonymous person or group going by the pseudonym Satoshi Nakamoto in the year 2008.

4.When was it invented?

Official Bitcoin was born on January 3, 2009. Its originator Satoshi Nakamoto mined the so-called "genesis block" into Bitcoin's blockchain - thereafter known as Block 0. The moment when the Bitcoin network came alive, everything that happened beforehand was just considered to be the prehistory by the cryptocurrency as we know it.

But the concept of Bitcoin was first made public several months in advance, on October 31, 2008, when Satoshi Nakamoto pre-released a so-called whitepaper entitled "Bitcoin: A Peer-to-Peer Electronic Cash System." Therein, he fully disclosed the underlying philosophy of Bitcoin, as well as its inner mechanics in some detail, including this idea of a digital currency not having any sort of intermediary in its transactions, such as a bank.

The later publishing of Bitcoin software in 2009, gave the world its first cryptocurrency. It is upon the bedrock of this whitepaper, and the later release of Bitcoin software in 2009, that the whole cryptocurrency industry was to be developed.

5.Who invented Bitcoin? What is a Bitcoin white paper?

Bitcoin was invented by a person or persons under the name Satoshi Nakamoto. The true identity of Satoshi Nakamoto has not yet been discovered to this date.

As far back as 2008, Satoshi Nakamoto published a whitepaper titled "Bitcoin: A Peer-to-Peer Electronic Cash System," which touted just what Bitcoin was and how it worked.

As it were, this Bitcoin white paper has brought into view the importance of the foundation in the crypto ecosystem:

The Bitcoin white paper is entitled "Bitcoin: A Peer-to-Peer Electronic Cash System." It is a nine-page seminal document, published by an anonymous author, using the pseudonym Satoshi Nakamoto

On October 31, 2008. It was in these nine pages that he gave Bitcoin its meaning, intention, and technical design: an innovative new form of decentralized digital currency able to perform peer-to-peer transactions well without assistance from any bank or other such bastion of trust.

Key Takeaways from the Whitepaper of Bitcoin:

1. Decentralized: The whitepaper postulates a system whereby the verification of transactions comes through a network of computers, otherwise known as nodes, and not some central authority. By default, that presents the system as resistant to control or manipulation.

2. Blockchain Technology: The idea of blockchain is basically based on this whole concept. It's a public ledger of all transactions kept in a process called mining, where miners solve complex cryptographic puzzles to validate and record transactions.

3. Proof of Work: This essentially sets up the logic whereby, to add any transaction to the blockchain as a block, miners do some computation; it actually secures the network.

4. The problem of double spending: The paper does address the double spending problem, which is the twin usages of the same digital cash, via a timestamp of blocks, in a cryptographically secure way.

5. Anonymity and Security: Transactions are pseudo-anonymous; therefore, the clients are represented via their open keys, which give users some privacy through not showing personal data.

It is commonly believed that the white paper of Bitcoin set the foundational elements of not only cryptocurrency but also blockchain, since it developed a new definition of money, transaction, and trust in the digital environment.

In 2009, Nakamoto released the first version of the bitcoin software that started up the network, mining the initial block, which came to be called the "genesis block" or Block 0.

He afterwards, continued to work on the Bitcoin project with other developers for a couple of years, while sending emails and communicating via online forums.

However, in 2011 he began to back away from the project and fade from public view, handing over the code repository and network alert key to other parties in the Bitcoin community.

From that moment, there were a lot of guesses regarding his identity, but his is still one of the biggest enigmas of the technological and financial world. People say that his name NAKAMOTO comes from the combination of already known names:

SAmsung and TOSHIba - SATOSHI.
NAKAmichi and MOTOrola NAKAMOTO.

In Japanese Satoshi means "clear thinking" or "quick witted", basically someone who is wised. The given name Nakamoto literally means "one who lives in the middle".

Also, in the crypto language Satoshi is used to refer to the smallest unit in BITCOIN being 0,00000001 (it is a one hundred millionth of a single bitcoin).
Although Satoshi Nakamoto signed the bitcoin whitepaper, it was impeccably written in English. Also, the way the author writes, mostly addressing himself as WE, not I, further made us reach to the conclusion that there must be a team behind the name.

6.What was it invented for?

Originally, cryptocurrency was targeted to be some form of decentralized, secure, and trustless money, independent of any government or banking central authority, deriving from the origin and concerns about the traditional financial system based on the use of central institutions to facilitate and control transactions. Some of the key reasons highlighted as to why cryptocurrency had been created are hereby stated:

1. Decentralization and Control
Traditional currencies usually depend on the regulation of central banks and governments and are normally subject to unshadow discretion in monetary supply and other indications. By their nature, starting from Bitcoin, all cryptocurrencies were created as decentralized, meaning not controlled by anyone. That was to give people more control over their money without the need for intermediary banks.

2. Transparency and Trust
Being based on blockchain technology, they guarantee transparency, given that each transaction is recorded in a public ledger. The implication of that fact is the ability for one to verify if a particular transaction ever took place without relying on any third party to prove such a thing. This removes the problem of the lack of trust that characterizes traditional finance, where the system thrives on corruption and mismanagement.

3. Safety
The cryptographic techniques secure the cryptocurrencies in such a way as to make them very hard to alter, forge, or even hack. All the consensus mechanisms therefore undergo a combination with this cryptographic security on the backbone of reducing fraud, double spending, and reducing cyberattacks.

4. Financial Inclusion
Indeed, the idea of currencies was part of the visions underlying cryptocurrencies: extending financial services to even unbanked or underbanked citizens. In cases where the traditional banking system is not that accessible, participation in cryptocurrency networks is easily allowed with access to the internet,

not taking so much effort, and one is allowed to conduct peer-to-peer transactions all over the world free of a bank account.

5. Abatement of the Charges Involved in Transaction and the Length of Time

Traditional financial systems take a lot of time, and, at times, money, to perform cross-border transactions. Cryptocurrencies try to make near-instant transactions with much lower fees, especially in the case of international transfers that are expensive and take considerable time conventionally.

6. Fighting Censorship, and Government Censorship

In some parts of the world, political or economic pretexts would drive their governments to go all the way to strict control over money movements or even account freeze. It is here that cryptocurrencies make themselves resilient to any form of censorship: one can just move his money around without any central authority obstructing this.

7. Hedging Against Inflation

For example, Bitcoin was meant to have a total supply of only 21 million coins, which would render it impervious to inflation through over-issuance, like fiat money that is printed willy-nilly by governments. This makes crypto sound stores of value in economies that are saddled with hyperinflation

8. Innovation in financial instruments

That has meant, in this context, the invention of cryptocurrency and an entirely new fashioning of systems and products of finance, like DeFi, allowing for completely new ways to lend, borrow, trade, and invest with no intermediary required. It has given birth to other classes of digital assets, including NFTs and decentralized autonomous organizations.

To put it simply, cryptocurrency was designed to be an alternative for the common systems of finance with a host of new features: decentralized, secure, transparent, accessible, and putting financial freedom in the hands of the individual.

7. How cryptos are created? What is mining, minting?

Cryptocurrencies are created during a process known as "mining" or "minting", depending on the kind of blockchain network and consensus mechanism set in operation. While there are a number of ways through which cryptocurrencies are mined, two of the most common mechanisms hitherto involved in the creation of cryptocurrencies are the Proof of Work and Proof of Stake.

Below highlights how each of these operates, among a few others:

1. Proof of Work (PoW) - Mining

- How it Works: Mining is basically the process whereby cryptocurrencies, such as Bitcoin for instance, are created. Miners engage in a race to solve complex mathematics by doing computational work. This adds to interconnected cryptographic functions that secure the blockchain.
- Block creation: The miner, once he has found the solution to the puzzle, validates a block of transactions added to the blockchain.
-Reward: This covers the reward to the problem solver or security provider to the network. Many times,

this is in the form of just-minted cryptocurrency, like Bitcoin; many other times, it consists of transaction fees.

Energy Consumption intensive: A great drawback with PoW is basically how intensive it consumes power; generally speaking, solving these cryptographic puzzles requires huge computational power. Example: Bitcoin, Litecoin.

2. Proof of Stake, POS - minting

- How it works: In Proof of Stake, validators will create new blocks and receive cryptocurrencies. Validators are randomly chosen depending on the number of cryptocurrencies owned by a validator and "staked" for a transaction. This system, unlike in computational power, is independent of the ownership of coins.
- Creation of Blocks: It selects validators to create new blocks and validates these kinds of transactions based on certain variables that include the number of coins one stake and the time for which one stake them.
- Reward: Most of the protocols give the newly minted coins to the validators for helping to secure the network apart from incentivizing through transaction fees.
- Energy efficiency: Well, the proof of stake is less energy-intensive since heavy computational work is not required.

Examples of this would be Ethereum post-Ethereum 2.0 when they switched over to PoS from PoW, Cardano, and Solana.

3. Delegated Proof of Stake (DPoS)

How it works: While different from PoS in this instance, users vote for a small number of delegates responsible for block validation and the security of the network; it can thus be termed a more centralized version of PoS.
- Block Creation: New block creation is performed by the delegates themselves. When the users vote for them, their role within the network is secured.
- Incentives: Validators are rewarded through transaction fees, block rewards, which they can share and distribute among the ones who voted for them.

 - Energy-efficient: DPoS is also efficient in terms of energy, as the number of block producers is limited. For instance, EOS and Tron are examples.

4. Mining in Centralized or Pre-mined Cryptocurrencies

Pre-mined or centrally issued: Some cryptocurrencies work in such a way that their total supply of coins is either created at the very start of a project, or by some central body, and later gets distributed.
- Block creation: No mining of the pre-mined coins or staking involved, and some or all the coins are pre-circulated in advance among the founders before the blockchain becomes a running concern.
- Pre-mine: There's no mining or staking reward since the coins already exist. Sometimes huge portions are kept by the owners or founders of the crypto coin.
Example: Ripple XRP, Stellar XLM.

5. ICO Development and Issue of Tokens on Already Existing Blockchains

Everything is designed in a way that developers can create new cryptocurrencies, so-called tokens, on top of existing blockchain networks, like Ethereum. Such tokens are usually launched through events, including the so-called Initial Coin Offerings (ICO's) or Initial DEX Offerings, where people buy tokens far in advance of their actual listing for public trading.

Token Standards: The majority of tokens created on Ethereum, for instance, are done on the ERC-20 standard. The majority of tokens do not have blockchains but instead use the security and infrastructure of the Ethereum Blockchain.

Example: Most of the DeFi tokens, including but not limited to, Uniswap-UNI, and Chainlink-LINK build up on the Ethereum Blockchain for its creation.

6. Forks of Pre-Existing Cryptocurrencies

- How it works: Most of the creation of new cryptocurrencies takes place in the form of a fork from the existing blockchain system. The fork is all about the alteration of the rules-the protocol alteration, to be specific-that result in the creation of a new version of cryptocurrencies that belong to different classes altogether.

Forks of those types are

Soft Fork: The soft fork is a minor update where the new version and old version of the blockchain can understand each other.

Hard Fork: It means that once some huge update appears, the blockchain forks into two blocks which after having the update, can't support each other and that's how another two new different cryptocurrencies appear.

Examples of this can be seen in the way Bitcoin Cash came about through a fork from Bitcoin and Ethereum Classic from Ethereum.

Conclusion

Cryptocurrencies can be created by mining, staking, pre-mining, and many other ways, or even the creation of tokens on an already existing blockchain. It, of course, depends on the consensus mechanism and what is targeted by the project of this cryptocurrency. Mining requires computational power, while staking is based on the principle of ownership and involvement in the security of the network. Other methods, like the so-called ICOs or forks, enable the issuance of tokens without developing a blockchain.

8.Mining of Bitcoin and minting of Cryptos:

It is mainly the process through which new Bitcoins are created, and at the same time, the means whereby the transactions come to be possible on the network. It involves finding the intricate mathematical puzzles necessary to add a new block of transactions to the Bitcoin blockchain, something important for recording all transactions within the network.

Key points relevant to mining in Bitcoin:

1. Proof of Work: Bitcoin mining employs a consensus algorithm called Proof of Work. Miners compete to find the solution to difficult cryptographic problems. The first one to solve the puzzle gets to extend the blockchain by adding the next block. This requires considerable computational power.

2. Block Reward: The block reward is what miners receive every time they mine and add a block into

the blockchain; this reward consists of freshly minted bitcoins.
This is a form of reward for miners, and it adds up to their means towards persuading them to further validate transactions.

Initially, the block reward was 50 Bitcoins, but the reward diminishes by half about every four years in an event also referred to as the "halving." Currently, the rate stands at 3,125 Bitcoins per block after the most recent halving that occurred back in April 2024.

3. Transaction Fees: Apart from the block reward, there are certain amounts as transaction fees that miners get from all those transactions that were included within the mined block. Correspondingly, as time goes by, when the block reward reduces by halving, it is supposed that transaction fees will make up much more of the miner's revenues.

4. Mining Difficulty: Every two weeks, due to the total computational power brought into the network, it automatically adjusts mining difficulty regarding the cryptographic puzzles. This adjustment ensures that, on average, one new block adds into the blockchain every 10 minutes.

5. Decentralization and Security: The whole idea in "decentralized" is that, theoretically, all participants with the proper equipment or software can mine. Just this very fact, makes the network much safer because it will be so difficult for any one participant to take control of the blockchain.

6. Energy Consumption: The process of mining Bitcoins involves powerful computation in order to solve these puzzles. Therefore, it involves great consumption of energy. Considering the consistent growth in size of the network, mining has, therefore, gained several criticisms for its ecological impact.

The Role of Mining:

-Transaction validation: Actually, what the miners do is validate the transactions at their insertion in a block, ensuring that the transactions are indeed valid according to the rules of the Bitcoin protocol, meaning not spending more than their balance and not sending money to a Ghost Address.
- Securing the Network: The mining process lets the Bitcoin network be secure because of how hard it is for an attacker to alter the blockchain. Assuming there has been an addition of a block; the alteration would require re-computation of its Proof of Work. Additionally, this implies redoing the Proof of Work of every block after it, which requires a great deal of computation.

This makes "mining Bitcoins" an activity considered to form the backbone, as it keeps the network of Bitcoins running.

Crypto Minting:

Minting in crypto refers to a process applied to create new cryptocurrency coins or tokens, usually within a blockchain network. This is one-way new units of cryptocurrency are generated and pumped into circulation. Its meanings vary with the specific blockchain type and consensus mechanism. The following section details how it works in different contexts:

1. Proof of Stake (PoS) Minting:
While similar in idea, different in concept, Proof of Stake systems define minting as the process of adding a new transaction onto the blockchain. Instead of racing to solve complex cryptographic puzzles like miners do in Proof of Work, in PoS, "validators"-an individual holding some stake in the network-can create new blocks depending on how much they hold and for how long they have held it.
PoS Mining: The validators "mint" by means of transaction validation and maintenance of network security. For that, they are given a certain portion of newly minted coins.

2. Minting of NFT:
Minting, regarding "Non-Fungible Tokens", is basically the creation of a unique digital asset on the blockchain. More precisely, it means that an artist or creator of an NFT is uploading a digital token with its special identity onto the blockchain and is proving the ownership of the token. The NFT remains on the blockchain forever and can be traded or sold.
NFT minting is the process by which digital arts, music, and other forms of expression are turned into some forms of digital and blockchain-based assets, majorly on such platforms like Ethereum, Solana, and Polygon.

3. Minting Tokens in New Projects:
New cryptocurrency projects mint their tokens in the creation phase. For instance, any time there is the introduction of a new DeFi or blockchain going into the market, the platform would normally mint some supply of tokens that users could get either by earning or buying. Of course, tokens do have other uses also, including providing the holder with governance rights, utility within a platform, and an investment class.
The typical asset: Initial Coin Offerings or Token Generation Events mostly are created on the basis of a fixed or flexible supply, with subsequent distribution among the investors or end-users.

4. Mining vs. Minting:
-Mining is a procedure carried out based on systems such as the Proof of Work system on Bitcoin, requiring the solving of complex puzzles with the aid of high-performance computers, where miners usually obtain rewards by the tender of newly minted coins.

- Minting: The general meaning includes something akin to issuing new coins due to the process of transaction validation without the need for intensive computational power.

Key differences:

- POW Mining: The miners will have to solve some pre-provided cryptographic problems. One such example is Bitcoin.

- POS Minting: through staking cryptocurrencies and creating the new blocks by way of transaction validation; in this case, most likely Ethereum 2.0.

NFT minting is the process of making exclusive digital content live on the blockchain.

Conclusion:
Minting in the crypto world refers to the creation of new tokens or coins, be it either through Proof of Stake mechanisms, NFTs, or token creation in new blockchain projects. Note that when people refer to minting, they almost always mean with the correct context, such as "with regards to NFTs," "POS mechanism," etc., since the process differs from one platform to another.

9.How to mine Bitcoin?

Mining Bitcoins involves some steps, and it does need special hardware, software, and somewhat tech-savvy persons to perform the tasks. The general overview goes this way:

1. Conquer the Basics
- Bitcoin Mining: It is the process by which computational power is applied to solve complex cryptographic puzzles, which, in turn, validate and secure transactions on the Bitcoin network. It, therefore, offers miners with an incentive in the form of newly minted Bitcoins together with the fees levied on transactions.

- Proof of Work: Bitcoins utilize the proof of work consensus algorithm, in which mining is employed through solving complex computations to create a new block in the blockchain.

2. The mining equipment should be purchased. ASIC Miners: An ASIC miner is, in essence, a device for mining Bitcoins and nothing else. Much more efficient than general-purpose hardware like CPUs or GPUs, these have now become standard tools for mining Bitcoins these days. Antminer by Bitmain and Whatsminer by MicroBT are two popular brands in the area of ASICs.

- Electricity: This venture needs an investment in loads of electricity to get the mining done. Consider the cost and availability in your area, since it may be one thing that will drive profitability.

3. Join a mining pool: Mining pools were formed when mining solo ceased to be a plausible mode of operation for the greater part, since the difficulty of mining one Bitcoin is very high. Miners would be creating what is called mining pools, wherein a few miners pool their computing power in order to raise their chance of solving a block. The reward that comes through the solving of a block is shared among the members in accordance with their contribution to the total hash rate of the pool.

- Popular Pools: There are several pools used in the mining process. Some of them are Antpool, F2Pool, and Slush Pool.

4. Install Mining Software: You will need to install a type of computer software that will allow your hardware to access the blockchain of Bitcoin and, if required, the mining pool. On Bitcoin, the most used mining software includes but is not limited to CGMiner, BFGMiner, and EasyMiner.

- Configuration: Your software needs to be configured pointing to the mining pool server. Mostly, it will be using pool credentials and your wallet to be used in acquiring a reward.

5. Setting Up a Bitcoin Wallet:

-Wallet: This is where the mined Bitcoins will come into. A Bitcoin wallet could be created for mobile or desktop, or it could be hardware-like-a Ledger or Trezor. Go for a wallet that has good security features.

- Address: Obtain a receiving address from your wallet, which you'll input into your mining software or mining pool account.

6. Begin Mining Monitoring: Now that everything's running, it's finally time to get into the nitty-gritty details. The performance of your miner, the payout from your mining pool, would be good. But most importantly, always check the temperature and energy consumption of your hardware, because overheating usually gets you a slowdown of the performance as a present. Maintenance: Upgrades your software and firmware periodically; clean your hardware from time to time; and, monitor the adjusting difficulty of your network.

7. Weigh the Costs

- Electricity: Mining can be electricity-intensive. Calculate your electricity cost in relation to potential rewards to find out whether it will pay off. Hardware Maintenance: ASIC miners also generate much heat; hence maintenance is quite vital to make sure it does not make it fail due to overheating.

-Mining Difficulty and Bitcoin Halving:

-the block reward gets cut by half every four years. This can be one influencing factor in profitability, so take your decision while keeping it in consideration.

8. Examine profitability

- Profitability Calculators: head to profitability calculators available for free online, like CoinWarz or WhatToMine. They'll estimate your earnings from mining based on your hardware, power costs, and current Bitcoin price and difficulty.

- Market Conditions: The price in Bitcoins is changing day by day; hence, mining profitability depends on it. Always keep tabs on the ongoing market trends and thereby create a strategy for the same.

9. Legal Outlook

- Regulations: First, learn about the legal status of mining Bitcoin in your country or region. Some cities or regions may have some regulations, given that enormous energy resources are consumed.

10. Look for other opportunities, Cloud Mining:

When setting up your mining rig becomes too complicated or expensive, you can opt for cloud mining: renting mining power from a service provider. With this, though you need to be doubly cautious of scams and untrustworthy providers.

Mining Altcoins: If competition in the mining of Bitcoin becomes very stiff it becomes wise that you mine other kinds of cryptocurrencies that have another algorithm, this will however be different both in hardware and the configuration in software. Mining of Bitcoins is very profitable and at the same time very costly; much investment, continuous maintenance, and minute detailing is required for profitable results.

10.What is Blockchain?

Blockchain is a decentralized, distributed, and digital ledger-based technology, recording all kinds of transactions on enough computers in such a manner that the registered transactions are retrospectively unable to be altered. The above is hereby explained in detail with respect to its key features and functionalities.

Key features

1. Decentralized: Unlike traditional databases, which are centralized in nature, a blockchain is maintained in a network of computers, or nodes in a blockchain, each having a copy of the whole blockchain.

2. Transparency: Since on-chain records are updated in real time on the chain and thus currently viewable by any viewer, this may engender a sense of trust among users and, perhaps, auditors.

3. Immutability: It is not possible to delete a transaction that has already been committed onto the blockchain, nor edit any detail that forms a part of that transaction. This is another aspect wherein every block gets linked to the previous one via cryptographic hashing, imbuing it with its immutable feature.

4. Consensus Mechanisms: Once some sort of consensus is achieved over the network by any mechanism, like PoW or POS, a new block is added to the blockchain. It provides a guarantee of an agreement at each node regarding the status of a set of transactions.

5. Security: Blockchain uses a number of cryptographic techniques to secure the data. Each block will have a unique cryptographic hash of the previous block, thus making a chain. For the same reason, it is virtually impossible to tamper with the data; if a malicious actor wants to change the data, it would require the alteration not only of that one block but of all the following blocks that need to be altered-taking the requirement of majority consensus on the network.

How It Works

1. Transaction creation: A new transaction is created and then broadcast on the network. Examples of information which can be part of this transaction are sender, receiver, and amount.

2. Verification of Transaction: Nodes in the network verify a transaction against a set of pre-defined rules. In other words, nodes verify that there are adequate funds covering the transaction, the balance is calculated right among many other various protocol-specific checks.

3. Block Creation: A cluster of transactions, once validated, gets added into a block. It would contain the summary of the transactions verified, the timestamp, and the hash of the previous block.

4. Consensus Mechanism: Other nodes on the network come to an agreement on the validity of the new block. In POW, every node that is competing tries to solve a given cryptographic puzzle; whoever solves it first has the block added in and receives a reward.

5. Block Addition: Once consensus is achieved, then the block is added to the blockchain. Each node of the entire network adds this block in its own copy of the blockchain.

6. Settlement: Once confirmed, no modification of a transaction is permitted, and the blockchain will be updated in front of all the participants of the network.

Applications of Blockchain

Cryptocurrencies are perhaps the best-known use, whereby blockchain acts as the backbone for cryptocurrencies like Bitcoin and Ethereum.

Smart Contracts: Contracts whose implementation is automated by coding the rules in lines of code, thereafter self-executing upon the fulfillment of certain conditions.
It will also raise the level of traceability and visibility in regard to supply chain activities.

Voting Systems: In some applications, it even allows for secret votes to be taken with openness.

Digital Identity: That's what it does; it provides for digital identity through safe validation.

Medical Care: Ensures the privacy of the patient's information among the practitioners in care.

The backbone of how cryptocurrencies work is the underlying blockchain technology. That is why its applications have broadened across industries on account of its security, transparency, and decentralized nature.

Cryptocurrency and blockchain are most assuredly associated with one another, yet it is very much possible to have cryptocurrencies that don't draw on a blockchain structure, at least conceptually speaking, in the traditional sense.

How it works, plus some alternatives:

1. Distributed Ledger
Block Chain is one type of Distributed Ledger, whereas all the Distributed Ledgers are not block chained. It is a decentralized data storage system that contains a record of several nodes. They may use some other methodologies to gain consensus or record transactions.
Example: 'IOTA' uses the so-called Tangle structure, a Directed Acyclic Graph-DAG, and not a blockchain. Transactions get confirmed in the case of confirmation from the network, yet it will not create a linear chain of blocks.

2. Hashgraph
Description: Hashgraph is another alternative to blockchain in some different ways, considering the different consensus algorithms. It is a kind of distributed ledger technology providing fast, fair, and secure consensus without mining.

Example: That will be the technology implemented on Hedera Hashgraph to enable very high transaction throughput at low latency.

3. Other Consensus Mechanisms

Description: Most other forms of cryptocurrencies and digital means realize their consensus mechanism in decentralization and security using other software methods, whereas some may be far different from the traditional blockchain-based systems.

- Example: 'Tendermint' is a great example of a consensus engine, utilized by projects such as Cosmos. It utilizes a Byzantine Fault Tolerance consensus algorithm, not a blockchain.

4. Central Bank Digital Currencies

Description: Digital Currencies or Tokens are not necessarily per se using decentralized ledgers. Some of them might be operated by one person or one organization within a traditional, centrally stored database.

An example could be that CBDCs, a form of money issued and controlled by the central bank of a country and may, therefore, have no block chain form but be centralized.

5. Hybrid Systems

Description: Some of these systems include blockchain, which can be combined with other technologies to optimize different needs: privacy, scalability, or speed.

Example: Chainlink integrates on-blockchain logic with off-blockchain data and services on-chain through oracles and is able to power smart contract functionality.

Overview/Conclusion

While blockchain is by far the more common, it is not the only possible underlying technology for a cryptocurrency. In this manner, other ways include distributed ledgers, hashgraphs, and other consensus algorithms through which such decentralized bookkeeping and recording of transactions can be obtained. Yet, blockchain has remained the general adopted and recognized framework for most cryptocurrencies due to its security and publicity already established.

11. Which came first, Bitcoin or blockchain?

While blockchain technology was developed right along with Bitcoin, Bitcoin was nevertheless a practical implementation of blockchain technology.

It came out as an idea for the first time in the Bitcoin whitepaper titled "Bitcoin: A Peer-to-Peer Electronic Cash System" by Satoshi Nakamoto in the year 2008. This whitepaper elaborated on how this underlying technology was utilized to power Bitcoin, a decentralized ledger while recording all transactions in the most secure manner.

The ideas themselves, such as cryptographic hashing, and so on, thus were around, but it wasn't until Bitcoin in 2009 that the first implementation came out. Both were basically born at about the same time; nevertheless, Bitcoin was the very first sort of application which brought the blockchain to life.

12.What is Blockchain, and what benefits does it have within a business?

What are the advantages of blockchain
Large-scale advantages relating to several industries and use cases are accorded by blockchain technology, hence making it very attractive. Some of the key advantages of blockchain are listed below:

1. Decentralization
No Single Point of Control: Because so many functions in a blockchain network of nodes are hugely decentralized, no one single power-government or corporation-can have any kind of control over the system, which makes it hard for the process to be manipulated.
The important thing in a peer-to-peer transaction is that it has enabled a user to deal directly with the other user in the transaction and is not necessarily dependent on the services provided by any intermediary, banks, or even a payment processor. It Reduces the dependency on third-party organizations hence lowers network transaction cost.

2. Immutability and Transparency
Public Ledger: This is literally the "public book" of all of the transactions which have ever occurred over the system. It is transparent to the entire set of participants making up the network. Everything is there for everybody to see, and it keeps them responsible by diminishing the probability of fraud.
Immutable Records: Once something has been added to the Blockchain, it is very hard to change or tamper with. This is why blockchains assure data integrity and hence find their ideal applications in auditing, supply chain tracking, or keeping legal records.

3. Safety
Safety of cryptographic security: Blockchain keeps the data in advanced cryptographic algorithms; hence, it's much resistant to any kind of hacking or unauthorized access to it. Each of these blocks has a link with the previously created block through a cryptographic hash. This simply means that in case some block needs to be changed, then all the subsequent blocks have to be changed, which is seriously computationally not viable.
Consensus Algorithm: Blockchain networks employ such consensus algorithms as POW or POS, which allow confirming the transactions in such a way that all participants of the network will further contribute to strengthening it by building one single picture of the ledger.

4. Cost cutting
This removes the intermediaries: Blockchain, allows peer-to-peer transaction that doesn't require any intermediary, like banks, brokers, and notaries. Thus, it reduces the transaction cost and speeds up the whole process.
Smooth Processes: Most processes had been automated by Blockchain. Smart contracts, therefore, reduce administrative costs in the execution of contracts and enhance efficiency in operations.

5. Speeding up the sales process
- Real-time or near-real-time settlement. That is because blockchain actually processes transactions in real time or near-real time, while for most traditional banking systems-considering lots of international

transactions-take as far as several days to finally settle on the books.
- 24/7: Most of the blockchains run 24*7, hence permitting performance of transactions at any given time with no restriction to business hours or else a particular time zone.

6. Better Trackability
- Supply Chain Transparency: The conditions of blockchain allow for the tracing of items within a supply chain from beginning to end. Each step of the process could potentially be written into the blockchain for all stages from the origin of a product right through to its finished state.
Anti-counterfeiting: the traceability feature of blockchain aids in proving the authentication of goods moving either from luxurious markets, pharmaceutical items, or even from the food supply chain, by helping get rid of risks for the penetration of counterfeit products into the system.

7. Smart Contracts and Automating
Since, after set conditions, computer programs will execute the activities of smart contracts automatically, then smart contracts can execute on their own. There will, therefore, not be the need to pay intermediaries in the form of lawyers and escrow agents, something that cuts down on time and money meant to be used in enforcing the contract.
It does bring efficiency in that it automates complicated workflows and processes, including those related to billings, dispute resolution, and insurance claims across diverse sectors.

8. Improved Privacy
Anonymity and Pseudonymity: Although blockchain is transparent, it can easily be used more anonymously or even pseudonymously. After all, one can operate with cryptocurrencies using their cryptographic addresses, not real-world identities. That way, the transactions would remain private and leakage of personal information avoided.
Selective Transparency: A private blockchain, if needed, for instance, can let an organization choose whom it grants access to the data and thus ensure confidentiality while still reaping the benefits of using blockchain technology.

9. Universal access
Financial Inclusion: Blockchain networking allows those unbanked and underbanked people who could not avail any financial facility to operate those now. In other words, due to blockchain networks, everyone who has access to the internet is included.
Cross-border Transactions: Blockchain has made it possible to carry out cross-border transactions without converting any currency, thus avoiding some of the most time-consuming procedures in traditional financial systems.

10. Robustness and Reliability
Decentralized Architecture: Because blockchain is decentralized, it would depend upon architecture, which may be distributed among thousands of nodes. The effective result is that it is highly resilient against attack or even system failure. If some of its nodes go down, the rest of the network can survive and keep working. No Single Point of Failure as with other systems that are centralized, like a crashing server or a hack, that may bring down the whole system. The good thing about blockchains, is that by design it actually resists such failures quite well.

11. Tokenization of Assets
Blockchain enables, a mechanism for tokenization (digitizing), the title of such real-world assets as land, real estate, art, and commodities on the blockchain. It enables partial ownership and, hence, improved liquidity and easy trading of such assets.
New Markets and Investment Opportunities: Tokenization through blockchain opens newer markets and creates more investment opportunities as, in the process, the hard-to-reach assets would have been made accessible to smaller investors too.

12. Data integrity and auditability
Tamper-Proof Data: Whatever gets recorded in the blockchain can hardly be tampered with. Thus, it assures data integrity over time; hence, it should be ideal for applications where regulatory compliances, medical records, and financial reporting are concerned.
Audit Trail: Blockchain keeps the record of the transactions in a widely available ledger that can be verified by all; this might turn out to be great with regards to audits and make accountancy errors or fraud less possible.

Conclusion
Advantages of Blockchain: decentralization, transparency, security, affordability, speedier transactions, and a whole host of other aspects that make the chain truly disruptive in industries related to finance, supply chains, and healthcare, among many others. Properties like these allow Blockchain to attain completely new levels of trust, efficiency, and accessibility to a wide range of participants in general.

How Blockchain Affects Business.
The impact that is being made on companies by cryptocurrencies and blockchain technologies is increasing in more diversified ways:

1. Modes of Payment: Other than the known forms of accepted payments, many businesses worldwide are now accepting using cryptocurrencies and against conventional modes of payment.

2. Investment and Fundraising: The sources are Initial Coin Offerings (ICO) or Security Token Offerings (STO) to raise capital. Plus, corporate strategies for some businesses are via investing in cryptocurrencies.

3. Integration of Blockchain: Blockchain is taken up by companies in order to integrate the same into various aspects of businesses, whether it be for supply chains, authentication of goods, or even for assurance of higher levels of transparency and security at each level of transaction being made.

4. Smart Contracts: Organizations implement smart contracts that automatically execute or enforce an agreement, without middlemen. This reduces many overheads and huge inefficiencies.

5. Decentralized Applications: Many companies create various blockchain platforms and then build decentralized applications on top of them for selling services or products in a very innovative way.

6. Cost-cutting: It drastically cuts the cost of transactions and time of processing the same, particularly those involving cross-border deals, when compared to traditional financial systems.

Cumulatively, cryptocurrency and blockchain are changing the very face of business: the way it operates, reaches customers, and most importantly, handles cash flow.

13. What are smart contracts?

A smart contract generally speaking is an agreement between multiple parties, expressed in a self-executing piece of code running on blockchain platforms; basically, it runs, performs, and enforces an agreement reached by the parties through express code, which is automated and intermediary-free. In a nutshell, how they do work and some of the key characteristics are brought out below:

Key Features

1. Automation
Description: Smart contracts will execute on their own when they reach a point of set criteria. This is an event that occurs without the interference of any human being.
- Example: Smart contracts execute automatically after providing a certain good, which is releasing the payment.

2. Decentralization
Description: Smart contracts are executed on blockchains, which makes them decentralized systems; this, in turn, translates to being distributed among a set of nodes, and hence they cannot be tampered with or censored.
Example: Ethereum Smart Contract executes on the Ethereum blockchain, whose nodes confirm and processes literally any kind of transaction.

3. Transparency
Description: Smart contracts represent pieces of code which are public, visible, and hence accessible on the blockchain. This feature also inherently makes them more transparent-their terms are clear, and more important, verifiable by all parties.
Example: This means that on Ethereum Blockchain, for example, anyone has a right to read the smart contract code in order to see what it is meant to do.

4. Immutable results
Description: Smart contracts are immutable in nature. Immutability, as the word suggests, means that once done, it cannot be modified. It means something which is set once, at the stipulation of the contract, and constant it remains, until modified by agreement.
Examples include that the on-chain deployed smart contracts to manage a token sale, can never be modified once deployed; meaning once a sale is setup, the terms can never be changed.

5. Safety
- Description: Smart contracts rely for their security on cryptographic algorithms of the underlying blockchain. It helps the contract avoid frauds or unauthorized changes.

Example, a smart contract involved in some form of virtual assets, would incorporate methods of cryptography to ensure that only the parties authorized could act on it.

How Smart Contracts Work

1. Writing Code
Description: Smart contracts are performed under a certain set of rules that have been codified into some program language intended for blockchain usage. For instance, something such as Solidity, intended for Ethereum.

Example: Code gives an example of development where a development provides conditions under which a payment is to be affected.

2. Deployment
Description: In the following example, deployment on a smart contract is made embedding a smart contract into a blockchain ledger.

- Example: The contract is consequently sent to the Ethereum blockchain, where it will be provided with an address in its name.

3. Interaction
Description: Interaction with the smart contract is realized by users sending transactions that would trigger its functions. Execution would follow the execution of the given input against the set of conditions given by the contract.

Example: A buyer pays some cryptocurrency into a smart contract; the smart contract confirms that, in fact, a payment took place and issues a digital asset to the buyer accordingly.

4. Implementation
Description: The smart contract, upon fulfilling the conditions, will execute the needed action automatically and record the same on the blockchain. Example: The contract, once the conditions of delivery have been met, pays off the money to the address of the seller.

Use Cases

1. Financial transactions - Description: Intermedial involvement is not required; it can automate bill payments, loans, and even insurance claims. - Example: The most common use cases in DeFi are the smart contract-based solutions for lending and borrowing.

2. Supply Chain Management Tracking and verification of goods on all movements to and through the supply chain. - Example: Smart contracts may automatically update the status of goods and may allow and trigger payments in respect of delivery.

3. Real Estate - Description: Assist in the selling and letting of properties, assist in dealing with their management. Example: A smart contract which represents the change of ownership and transfer of money during the sale of real estate.

4. Digital Identity Description: Verification or authentication of an individual's identity and credential over the network. Example: One of the various applications is the issuance of smart contracts that imply verification and permission for access to digital services.

5. Governance Ability to enable the handling of such a process type, such as voting and decision making by decentralized organizations. Example: smart contracts can be used for managing, handling funds on behalf of the Decentralized Autonomous Organization.

Smart contracts represent a quantum leap in methods of making and maintaining agreements with the use of blockchain technology. It uses the blockchain to automate applications in a very transparent and secure way.

14..What are Proof of work (POW) and proof of stake ? (POS)?

Proof of Work is a consensus algorithm in most digital currencies, especially applied to Bitcoin, which helps to keep the network secure and validate any transaction with the help of complex mathematic puzzles needing huge computation and energy. The underlying process works as follows:

1. Mining: This is a process where many miners compete to solve a cryptographic puzzle. This is computationally intensive, easy to verify once the solution has come out, and usually means finding a hash, and meeting particular criteria.

2. Verification and Confirmation about a solution: in case of a found solution, the right to add one more block of transaction into the Blockchain and the Solution found is sent into the network, where the correctness will be checked by other miners.

3. Incentives: The successful miner gets a reward in terms of freshly minted cryptocurrency, apart from the transaction fees of the transactions included within the block.

4. Security: This puzzle is so computationally expensive to solve that this also discourages an attacker who wishes to rewrite the blockchain, because one would have to redo the proof of work for every subsequent block in a very implausible manner.

While this has sought to decentralize networks with blocks, it is always criticized because of the power it consumes in POW and generally because of its effects on the environment.

Besides the proof-of-work mechanism, there are different consensus mechanisms, among them, the so-called proof of stake. In other words, the proof of stake in cryptocurrency refers to a consensus algorithm that demands those who perform validation, "stake" or "lock up", some portion of their holding of that cryptocurrency so that they are allowed to create a new block. Accordingly, validators in creating blocks are chosen based on the amount of cryptocurrency they possess instead of being chosen based on their computational power.

1. Staking: In POS, validators are part of the process of validating transactions, chosen in proportion to the number of coins a given validator holds and that are agreed to be "staked" for a given period (as collateral). Therefore, the higher the number of coins staked, the greater the chance to create the next block.

2. Validation: A validator confirms a transaction and adds a new block to the chain. POS doesn't need to have very complex computations; hence, it is energy-efficient.

3. Rewards: Very often, validators are rewarded after the confirmation of any block usually in the form of transaction fees or additional cryptocurrency. In case some validator acts dishonestly, then they could get slashed-a certain part of their staked coins being taken away-which once more incentivizes good behavior.

4. Security: On the level of design itself, POS is energy-efficient and highly scalable than POW. In this case, security is given because of economic incentives: bad behavior by some validator can be penalized with the partial or complete losing of the staked coins.

The use of cryptography by various digital cryptocurrencies is implemented via the Proof of Stake consensus algorithm, including Ethereum, which joined the list after the migration from POW to the proof-of-stake consensus mechanism, further joined Cardano and Polkadot. This is preferred in use because it consumes less power and promises faster times in the time of transaction processing.

15.What is the minimum value of Bitcoin that I can purchase?

The smallest unit of Bitcoin, called Satoshi, is the fraction in which one can buy Bitcoin. That one Bitcoin is divisible to 100 million Satoshi and has been made equivalent to 0.00000001 BTC. In most instances, however, exchanges have set their minimum purchase amount, usually from $1 to $10 of Bitcoin.

How it generally works is this:
Exchanges: Major exchanges in the cryptocurrency market, like Coinbase, Binance, and Kraken, allow users to buy very small fractions of Bitcoin. They, on the other hand, commonly have minimum buys in fiat currency, like USD or EUR, with some being as low as $10.

Fees: Keep in mind that buying very small amounts might incur relatively high transaction fees, which can affect the value of your purchase.
So, technically you can buy as little as 0.00000001 BTC, but in the real world, that minimum depends on the platform you're using and, secondly, the transaction fees involved.

16.Adoption of Cryptos today

Adoption of cryptocurrency is not the same across borders, as different regions and different industries take more to crypto in their own respective ways. Where and how crypto is getting adopted today:

1. Adoption by Geography:
- North America:
- United States: In the U.S., there are a considerable number of users, exchanges, and businesses that take cryptocurrency. Most of the major towns are slowly developing into crypto centers. For instance, New York and Miami are mainly huge business cities, where most of the businesses have started to adopt Bitcoin among many other cryptocurrencies.
Canada: The government of this country has embraced cryptocurrency regulation in a very friendly manner; hence, crypto application in various spheres like paying and investment is widely used, and full Bitcoin ATMs maintain their pace.

- Europe:
- Germany treats Bitcoin as legal tender, and most businesses already welcome it for all kinds of different payments. Berlin is considered one of the focal points of crypto-friendly attitude and leniency in regulation.
- Switzerland: With the so-called "Crypto Valley" located in Zug, Switzerland, this is another major hub of innovation for both Blockchain and Cryptocurrency, considering how many companies and projects are residing therein.
Owing to the uses adopted for financial services, settling means, and as a form of investment, the United Kingdom houses the growing market of cryptocurrencies.

- Asia:
Japan: most likely has the friendliest crypto laws, clear regulation, and wide acceptance of Bitcoin for retail purposes both in real life and online.
- South Korea: Cryptocurrency adoption in South Korea is very high, especially for trading and investment purposes. In a broad sense, any kind of use case involving blockchain technology has interest in one way or another.
Some of the centers of crypto exchanges, blockchain startups, and pioneering finance services employing crypto are based in Singapore.

- Latin America:
El Salvador: Well, nobody expected this, but El Salvador became the first country ever which adopted Bitcoin as legal tender in 2021. The Government of El Salvador has already aligned Bitcoin in its economy. It has installed Bitcoin ATM machines, government wallets, and forced many merchants to accept Bitcoins.
While the Brazilian government is still in contemplation mode regarding the issuance of its own CBDC, use cases have gone up in remittances, through payments, and by investment in what is a budding crypto market.

- Africa:
Nigeria: Being one of the most advanced adopters of cryptocurrencies on the African continent, having a youthful population, coupled with its remittances and shaky economy means that volumes passing through in peer-to-peer trades are sizeable.
It came in view that, among other countries, South Africa was one of the countries that marked a fast-growing crypto user base, firms, accelerated e-commerce adoption, and a rise in investments.

- Middle East:
United Arab Emirates: The UAE is turning into a crypto hub, mainly Dubai, having very friendly regulations that strongly increase the number of exchanges and blockchain projects.

2. Adoption at Sector level:
- Finance: The following may be done with the aid of eToro:

Trading and Investment: Cryptocurrencies are treated as an investment asset, so their trading is done very actively by exchanges, brokers, and institutional investors.

- DeFi or Decentralized Finance:

DeFi opens possibilities with regards to the dispersion of traditionally intermediated financial services by means of lending, borrowing, and yield farming.

- E-commerce:

Many allow the buying of a product using Bitcoin, Ether, amongst others and stablecoins on other online retailers or other platforms; the most prominent ones include Overstock, Newegg, and shops powered by Shopify.

- Remittances:
It is positioning itself fairly fast for cross-border remittances, allowing cheaper fees, and faster than what traditional banking systems are capable of handling, especially in parts of the world where banking is not well established.

- Real Estate:
Some allow the sale of their properties for cryptocurrency in exchange for those sales. A number of major purchases have taken place in the U.S., Dubai, and Europe.

- Gaming and Digital Goods:
Examples of usage cases of such cryptocurrencies and tokens would include rewards, in-game purchases, and digital collectibles considered as NFTs; hence, these are intended in the gaming industry. Examples of crypto-based gaming ecosystems include Axie Infinity and Decentraland.
NFT stands for Non-Fungible Tokens.
NFTs are everywhere: with respect to music, art, and the entire entertainment industry, artists and creators have started reaping revenues through the sale of various forms of digital assets or collectibles on online marketplaces such as OpenSea and Rarible.

-Charitable Giving and Philanthropy
Some of the uses of cryptocurrency also include increased donations, which are facilitated by organizations such as The Giving Block for charities and nonprofits to accept cryptocurrency donations.

Conclusion
In other words, adoption is taking place across boards, not with equal speed across countries and sectors. Be it, leading regions in terms of regulation clarity or enterprise-wide business acceptance, digital cryptocurrencies find their place within a host of sectors, including but not limited to finance, e-commerce, and real estate.

17..Crypto adoption since creation
F-rom nameless technology to mainstream financial innovation, crypto adoption has come a long way since Bitcoin was created in 2009, and the journey has made its way through certain consequential

phases:

1. Early Days: 2009 to 2012
-Creation of Bitcoin: Bitcoin was considered the first cryptocurrency, created in 2009 by a person or group of people under the pseudonym of Satoshi Nakamoto. It was a new form of money that strove to be utterly decentralized-with no central authority.
-Initial Fervor in the Minds of Geeks: A few cryptographers, programmers, and libertarians as early adopters, fascinated with the idea of decentralized money. Bitcoin was used in some select online communities, not in the real world.
- First Real-World Transaction: Bitcoin had its very first real-world transaction in the year 2010, in which a programmer, Laszlo Hanyecz, paid 10,000 BTC in return for two pizzas. This is still celebrated annually today as "Bitcoin Pizza Day.".
-Exchanges Emerged: For instance, Mt. Gox went online in 2010, thus allowing people to begin a wider adoption through exchanging Bitcoin for traditional currencies.

2. Growth and Diversification 2013-2016
-Once Bitcoin was up and running, many other cryptocurrencies, now referred to as altcoins, began to emerge. One of the very early generation altcoins was Litecoin, which was developed in 2011. Further down the chain with even greater capabilities and uses are: Ripple as XRP, Ethereum as ETH, and Dogecoin as DOGE.
-Silk Road and Early Use Cases: Bitcoin first came into prominence due to its use on Silk Road, an online marketplace for everything from heroin to Glock pistols, shut down by the FBI in 2013. Events of this type made clear that the potential of cryptocurrencies would, in equal measure, run hand in hand with challenges.
-Higher media attention and increased volatility of the price: the price increase of Bitcoin in 2013 was very rapid, drawing massive media attention. Many more investors entered into the coin, including traders who would buy and then immediately sell their coins. This also had the effect of increasing the price volatility in Bitcoin. For the times when the prices are extremely high, there is a high possibility of great crashes in value.
- Ethereum and Smart Contracts: Ethereum went live in 2015. With it came smart contracts, which let developers build applications-mostly dApps-on top of its blockchain network. This opened further prospects for the blockchain beyond just plain-old transactions.

3. Mainstream Attention and the ICO Boom (2017-2018):
-The Bull Run of Bitcoin: During 2017, its price kept on climbing, nearly touching $20,000 by the end of that year. This underlined for the very first time how cryptocurrencies can pull in a humongous amount of retail and institutional interest.
- Initial Coin Offerings: The first 2017 boom saw a stream of new projects issue their tokens on Ethereum and other platforms to raise money. Many investors wishing to join the exponential growth of leading cryptocurrencies succumbed to numerous failures and scams in that very year.
Regulatory Scrutiny: The sudden growth of cryptocurrency projects swept across the face of regulators across the world; countries like China banned the creation and trading in digital currency, while other countries started work on the development of frameworks that would outline a system to regulate the growth of the emerging market.

4. Market Maturation and Institutional Involvement - 2019-2020

-Market Correction and Stabilization: Immediately after the 2017 bull run came the 2018 great correction, where most tokens lost almost all their value. In respect, that was the maturation of the market, where people started focusing on longer-term projects, with much more sustainable growth. Increased institutional interest was developed in cryptocurrencies, with big financial institutions and companies investing in them. Companies such as Fidelity introduced crypto custody services, and the first Bitcoin futures appeared on conventional exchanges.

-DeFi - Development: Indeed, in the years 2019 and 2020, one could finally see maturity when some platforms actually started offering, among other things, the possibility of lending and borrowing money in a decentralized fashion on such systems. This growth has shown just how ready blockchain technology was to break into traditional financial services.

5. NFTs go into the Mainstream Adoption: 2021 - Present

-Legality: El Salvador is the first country that recognized Bitcoin as legal tender, doing so for the first time in 2021, and it has seen the most mileage with respect to mainstream adoption around the world.

-NFT Mania: NFTs are non-fungible tokens that became very popular in 2021. Digital art, collectibles, and even virtual land began to sell for millions in them. A new kind of audience went into the crypto space-for instance, artists, musicians, and gamers.

-Corporate Adoption: Large corporations such as Tesla, Square, and MicroStrategy entered the world of Bitcoin with great fanfare. The integration of cryptocurrency services had begun to take shape-even huge payment processors such as PayPal and Visa began integrating cryptos

-CBDCs: Several governments worldwide started to do research on and develop their forms of digital currencies. Among these, China has been quite proactive in testing its form of a digital yuan, although most of them, like the US and the EU, work on research into possible ways of using them.

-Regulatory Focus: Ever since digital money started getting all the public eye, there have been variants of attempts by different regulators globally to try and bring better clarity with respect to crypto assets. Consumer protection, AML, and tax compliance, all make the hot topics to variant lists.

6. Current Trends

-Web3 and Decentralized Apps: The concept of Web3, till date, was supposed to be a decentralized version of the internet which would work on a blockchain backend. It will also involve developing decentralized social networks, data storage solutions, and digitized identity systems.

- Entrance into the Metaverse: More and more, cryptocurrency and blockchain technology find their place in building the metaverse with its virtual worlds and digital economies, constituted by tokens and NFTs.

-Environmental Concerns and the Push for Sustainable Blockchain Solutions: As the ecological footprint by blockchain technologies has gained momentum, awareness has been paid to constructing more environmentally viable solutions. Major changes include Ethereum's change to proof-of-stake and new blockchains that are more eco-friendly.

Conclusion

In such a way, the adoption of cryptocurrency has moved from an esoteric, technology-driven experiment to a full-fledged, global financial movement,one that speaks to a very different future of money, finance, and indeed technology. Not to say that challenges no longer exist, from regulatory uncertainty to market volatility, to name just two. But the trend toward broader industry- and geography-based adoption remains on an upward trajectory.

18..Will crypto replace money as we know it?

Whether cryptocurrency will replace traditional money as we know is a quite complex argument, depending on a set of different economic, technological, regulatory, and social factors. Below are the main arguments both supporting and opposing to such a possible eventual shift:

The reasons for and against cryptocurrency taking the place of regular money are below.

1. Decentralization and Control

By their very nature, digital cryptocurrencies fully exclude the respect of the role of middlemen in the regulation of transactions. Digital cryptocurrencies are to stay in the circle of decentralized systems, apart from any middleman, central bank, or government regulating money supply. The above fact ensures personal financial sovereignty, wherein an individual controls his or her money directly, free from intermediaries

Resilience to Inflation: Most cryptocurrencies, such as Bitcoin, possess capped supplies, making them resistant to those inflationary policies that reduce the value of fiat money in case the central banks print excess money.

2. Borderless and Global Accessibility

Financial Inclusion: The concept of cryptocurrencies was to enable everyone to enter into the world economy whereby mainstream banking was not accessible. Crypto offers the unbanked or underbanked populace a mean of a store of value and a method of transferring it independently from banks.

Cross-border transactions: Using cryptocurrencies allows for the precise and immediate transfer of cash across borders at very low costs. This is vastly different from classic banking, in processes that may take a number of days and are considerably expensive in cross-border settlements.

3. Safety and Clarity

Immutable Ledger: The ledger nature in blockchain is open and indelible. This reduces fraudulent practices and corruption by its very nature. This has found application in high-value financial transactions for example, where the reliance on third-party verification is less.

Being of a cryptographic nature, virtual currencies could not be counterfeited; therefore, making them safer to use as media of exchange than even physical cash.

4. Programmability: Smart Contracts

The Fully automated financial processes, by means of smart-contract-supporting cryptocurrencies like Ethereum, will eliminate the need for a human intermediary in tracking performances-from payments to insurance claims-and in the process, make the entire financial system much more efficient and reliable.

5. Transition into an Economically Digital Society: The more of the global economy that becomes digital, the easier cryptocurrencies might go through a world in which goods, services, and money are increasingly transacted online. Digital currencies would at least fit better into an online economy than physical cash does.

Opposition's reasoning for not replacing traditional money with cryptocurrency:

1. Regulatory and Governmental Resistance

-Government Control of Money Supply: As a matter of fact, there are strong reasons why governments would not want to give up control of their independent currencies, using the same as leverage in monetary policy, tax collections, and general economic stability. Cryptocurrencies have been designed in a way to take away this particular leverage, and that is yet another probable source of opposition from these vested interests.

Legal and Regulatory Hurdles: These are in the form of many different kinds of regulatory challenges faced by cryptocurrencies and, of course, becoming a challenge to comply completely with AML and CTF legislation. Another area in which governments can make a difference is through setting adverse regulations on the great adoption of cryptocurrencies as CBDC.

2. Prevalence of Volatility without Stability

    Volatility: Cryptocurrencies are highly volatile. Although Bitcoin has been termed a virtual store of value, the fluctuation in its value might be felt within very short lengths of time. This kind of volatility makes it completely unfit for daily use, where predictability of price is vital. It is not predictable with regards to monetary policy. Most conventional currencies have provisions for monetary policy while the central bank ensures that it is predictable for the sake of controlling inflation. However, cryptocurrencies, in this case a decentralized virtual currency like Bitcoin, do not have any controls that might be hazardous in financial environs.

3. Scalability fused with speed in transactions

    Blockchain Scalability Problem: Most of the blockchain networks, especially older generations like Bitcoin and Ethereum, have scalability issues in one way or another when it comes to transaction speed. High congestion of the network raises fees, slowing down transaction times; hence, that makes cryptocurrencies a little less effective for wide usage compared to the existing mechanisms of making payments.

    Energy Consumption: Some cryptocurrencies are seriously power-consuming, with the mains being POW. An example could be Bitcoin. Considering ecological sustainability as being rather important in the contemporary world, this could be one of the factors that acts as a deterrent to its mass adoption.

4. User Experience and Understanding

- Complexity to everyday users: While cryptocurrency aficionados do not mind using digital wallets, managing private keys, and surfing blockchain networks; to the great unwashed masses, such processes are dauntingly complex and fraught with risk. In other words, if wide diffusion had taken place, interfaces would have to be more usable and education improved.

- Loss of Access: Misplacing a private key by a cryptocurrency investor would likely translate to the loss of access to those resources forever. That is not exactly how traditional banking works, where, on most occasions, one can recover a lost credential.

5. Adoption and Trust

-Centrality and conventional institutions: Whereas conventional banking systems have lost confidence, it is trusted that belief in central banks and government-backed money is still intact. Any shift of this would definitely mark a big change on cultural and economic grounds for societies that have immense faith in the centralized system.

-Resistance to Change: Crypto-currency would require an overall embracing of change in the mindset of the masses in terms of how they perceive and use money. Most people are very reluctant to switch over to another system especially when the financial systems in their countries are stable and work efficiently. Probably the hybrid future, in which crypto exists with conventional money.

-Central Bank Digital Currencies: The very concept of the issuance of Central Bank Digital Currencies, a mix of both cryptocurrencies in aspects like digital transactions, with the stability and regulations of fiat, is an idea some governments are working on. It would more plausibly be a bridge connecting traditional money with completely digital currency, than one replacing either.

Niche applications of cryptocurrencies would be where?

On one hand, cryptocurrencies cannot fully replace traditional money, but probably their niche could be in international remittances, in DeFi, or even uses for a store of value, such as "digital gold" in the case of Bitcoin. These, for those purposes, would augment and not necessarily replace the current financial systems.

Conclusion: Among the benefits of the cryptocurrencies over traditional money are decentralization, security, and the possibility of crossing borders. However, volatility, regulatory obstacles, and scalability decrease any expectation that in the near future, traditional money would be wholly replaced by cryptocurrencies. Probably, one more plausible prospect is the coexistence of cryptocurrencies together with the fiat currencies, whereby the governments themselves might declare their version of digital currencies, namely CBDCs, in order to reap the benefit of blockchain technology while retaining their control of the monetary system.

19..Who uses crypto today, and who will use it tomorrow?

Entities that currently use cryptocurrencies range from simple individuals to companies, governments, and even international organizations. Most predict that the rate of the adoption of the cryptocurrency will increase even further in the years to come. These current and future crypto users can be differentiated through a number of needs and motivations, including for investment, for transaction, and technological innovation.

Who is using cryptocurrency today?

1. Retail Investors and Speculators
    Motivation: Cryptocurrencies like Bitcoin and Ethereum are usually targeted by individual investors who are speculative in nature. Their speculation is to probably gain profits from appreciation or speculate with short-run trading.
    Among them, the most famous ones are Bitcoin, or in shortened form BTC, Ethereum, which is known as ETH, and the so-called altcoins-for example, Solana, DOGE, or Dogecoin, and many others.
    Geographical Distribution: The investors are dispersed over the globe, resident in most of the great financial markets of the world, such as the United States, South Korea, Japan, and parts of Europe.
2. Institutional Investors
    Large investment funds, hedge funds, and asset management companies are positioning more and more cryptocurrency in their portfolio. In general, for some large investors, crypto's an inflation hedge, a type of "digital gold," while for other investors, it is a class of assets with very high growth potential.

These are key players that include firms like Grayscale and MicroStrategy, while major investment firms such as BlackRock have started offering crypto-related products, or holding the cryptocurrency on their balance sheet.

- Future Growth: Institutional investment is on the rise, coupled with clarity over regulations of traditional financial players and confidence in the infrastructure of cryptocurrencies.

3. Tech-savvies and developers who are interested in the latest trends.

Motivation: The people who are majorly into cryptocurrencies are blockchain developers, coders, and generally tech-savvy people, given that they actually put their cryptocurrencies into work by developing dApps, studying smart contracts, and generally participating in blockchain ecosystems. They are amongst the very first users of new blockchain platforms like Solana, Polkadot, and Ethereum Layer 2 solutions.

- Common Uses: Tech-savvy users interact with decentralized finance (DeFi) platforms, NFT (non-fungible token) marketplaces, and engage in crypto mining and staking.

4. Unbanked and underbanked communities

Motivation: The general thinking is that cryptocurrencies serve as an alternative means of storing value, a means of making payments, and a channel to other financial services, where the traditional banking channel is unavailable or expensive. As such, this happens to be seen mostly in countries where the financial infrastructure is quite weak or those suffering from high inflation.

The prominent examples here are cryptocurrencies, being highly utilized by classes of people that cannot afford to access financial facilities in countries like Nigeria, Venezuela, and most parts of Southeast Asia and Africa.

- Use Cases: Cross-border payments, savings, and settling among friends and family with the use of stablecoins or other cryptocurrencies such as Bitcoin.

5. Traders and Businessmen

Motivation: Many businesses already accept cryptocurrencies in lieu of their goods and services, either in trying to reach or sell to a more technologically savvy customer segment, or because transaction fees accompanying such systems are less than those offered by big networks such as Visa or Mastercard.

Examples include Tesla, Overstock, and Shopify merchants in some markets, all of which accept crypto for payment. Crypto payment processors such as BitPay and Coinbase Commerce also provide the functionality.

Other industries accepting crytos include the industries of e-commerce, technology, and even some real estate and luxury items allowing cryptocurrency as modes of payment.

6. Decentralized Finance (DeFi) Users

Motivation: DeFi allows users to lend, borrow, trade, and earn on interest through blockchains without any middleman from traditional finance. Respective cryptocurrencies are used to achieve liquidity, yield farming, or DEX for this purpose.

Platforms: Applications like Uniswap, Aave, and Compound all run on Ethereum and other blockchains.

7. Governments and Central Banks - In its Experimental Stages

Motivation: Through the adoption of cryptocurrency, be it Bitcoin adoptions like in El Salvador or the making of their Central Bank Digital Currencies, governments finally seem to understand a means to renew themselves toward the modern age in the use of money and simultaneously control said money.

Notable Examples: Its use as legal tender in El Salvador; the central bank of China tested a digital yuan, the e-CNY. Many other countries are also already launching or studying CBCDs, including Sweden and the Bahamas.

But who are the people that, later on, will use cryptocurrency?

1. Mainstream Consumers

Motivation: As utilities go up and there is better adoption of cryptocurrencies in life, they could be utilized by mainstream consumers to keep the score on payments, savings, and finally to prove one's digital identity.

Possible Growth: Crypto-friendly mobile applications, stablecoins, and the improvement in User Interface, will help in getting everyday consumers on board. Some of the very important integrations that has been done with popular financial applications such as PayPal to Square hint at consumer adoption in the near future.

2. Large enterprises and multinational companies

Motivation: Large enterprises will use cryptocurrency in the management of treasury, cross-border payments, and decentralized finance in the future. They can also apply the benefits of blockchain technology in the monitoring of their supply chain, data storage, and the creation of smart contracts. Such use cases that are normally pointed out include holding crypto on their balance sheets, creating internal token ecosystems, receiving crypto payments, and using blockchain for logistical tracking.

3. Governments and Central Banks: Mass Adoption

Motivation: More and more governments are likely to make their minds up for the introduction of their CBDCs, with a view to retaining the controlling powers of the monetary system in the face of the digital economy. Unlike, for instance, bitcoin, the new digital currencies will be state-backed, using blockchain technology, hence guaranteeing swift and secure transactions.

Examples include the fact that in the future, CBDC could always coexist with cryptocurrencies in a decentralized manner from the United States, the European Union, or other bigger economies.

4. Less Developed Nations: Improvement in Financial Inclusion

Crypto is going to continue with its important role of offering the unbanked in developing nations access to financial means. As more have access online, and crypto wallets are easier to use, more will begin using crypto in daily life.

Crypto-stablecoin and local blockchain solutions for remittance, mobile payments, and savings will most likely increase in use in the near term, as countries with high inflation levels and inadequate access to banking are in dire need of alternatives.

5. Content Creators and Digital Artists: NFT Growth

Motivation: The reason behind this is that it opens up a whole new avenue of revenue streams available for the digital content creators, musicians, and digital artists alike. In the future, NFTs will make up much more significant proportionate parts of the digital economy than at the present time, and therefore the creators may have great opportunities for monetizing their works directly without necessarily having to go through the middlemen.

- Application of NFTs automatically goes beyond art, in fields such as gaming, land, and even patent applications.

6. DAOs - Decentralized autonomous organizations
Motivation: A DAO is a concept of an ownerless organization, something like automated associations, running on a written code called a smart contract, or by voting among its community members, many times funded by cryptocurrencies. Later on, companies will start transforming into DAOs with regard to decision-making and financial issues.
Adoption: By the time the given legislative protection has come into being, many more will be practicing forms of decentralized self-management, new collaborative funding models.

7. Virtual Economies and the Metaverse
Value: Since the idea of the metaverse is growing, this might occupy a very important role in the virtual world of base currency. People will be buying or selling goods, services and digital real estate using crypto.
Crypto tokens will be utilized to power decentralized social networks, virtual games, or virtual-Reality-like platforms, better known as metaverses, examples of which include but are not limited to Decentraland and The Sandbox.

8. Non-Governmental Organizations (NGOs) and Charities
More so, there is increased capacity through which charities and NGOs would accept donations and dispense such monies in a very transparent manner using cryptocurrencies. In this regard, the utilization of the blockchain is quite important in ensuring the transparency of all donations.
- Use cases: Crypto can route around corrupt financial systems to facilitate international NGOs or be used directly as a peer-to-peer method of paying in crisis situations.

Conclusion:
Today, cryptocurrency is used by a varied population of retail and institutional investors, developers of technology, and the less acknowledged areas of the population in developing regions. Once it becomes more advanced and integrated into the mainstream, mainstream consumers, governments, and large corporations will also most likely find more ways to use crypto. It would be about increased adoption in DeFi, digital art, and virtual economies, yet the usage associated with a cryptocurrency for financial inclusion and cross-border transactions is going to be far more relevant.

20..Is Crypto available to all?

Theoretically, yes, it is accessible for every person connected to the Internet, but the situation looks quite different when variables like technological infrastructure, economic conditions, and regulatory environments of the countries in question come into account, as well as the background of the individuals. Now, let me describe it in detail:

1. The Usage of the Internet and Technology.
Internet Access: Cryptocurrencies cannot be used sans the use of the internet. Now, this may be something that seems already given to people living in developed regions, but for a fact, there are parts of the world that do not have this facility, or for that matter, it may be highly limited and restricted to

major cities, leaving the rural and underdeveloped areas lagging.

Device Availability: Operating cryptocurrencies requires one to have either a smartphone or a computer to interact with wallets, exchanges, and dApps. Most people of undeveloped nations lack the means or ability to gain these devices and therefore are cut off from accessing crypto.

2. Financial Literacy and Education

Knowledge and Understanding: Cryptocurrencies may be quite complicated even for those people who have some experience in areas of finance or working with digital technologies. Wallet management, protection of private keys, and at least partial understanding of how blockchain works; all that requires specific computer literacy, which not everybody possesses.

Risk Awareness: Most have no idea how to handle the volatility, fraud, or the impossibility of returning a transaction once it has been put on a blockchain endemic in digital currencies. Without proper education in this aspect, a newcomer can make extremely costly mistakes.

3. Obstacles to Regulation

Legal Barriers: Some countries ban cryptocurrencies, putting many restrictions in place courtesy of governments. For example, some nations, like China, have banned crypto trading and mining, putting limits on their citizens' access. Most countries are still working to clearly outline regulations, leaving everything up in the air.

Regulatory Compliance: Even in those countries that allow the operation but with regulation, the process makes the owners go through strict verification processes, with the Know Your Customer (KYC), to be able to access an exchange. Such efforts are going to continue in ways that will cut off any path to crypto-assets for those kinds of people, who do not own required identification or means of banking.

4. Banking and Payment Gateways

Access to Banking Systems: Whereas they are, for the most part, engineered to work without mainline banks, the process of buying cryptocurrency tends to involve attaching a bank account, debit, or credit card, especially when using more centralized exchanges like Coinbase or Binance. The friction among budding crypto adopters certainly includes not being plugged into such systems in the first place.

Fiat Onramps: In some countries, the ability to convert any Fiat currency (that is, conventional money, such as the USD, EUR, etc..) into cryptocurrency and vice-versa, can be a problem. In countries with only a few payment gateways, or where banks fail to support the transaction in cryptocurrency, buying or selling crypto is quite hard.

5. Financial Barriers

Transaction Fees: Whereas virtual currencies claim to have lower transaction costs, some online networks like Bitcoin and Ethereum charge pretty exorbitant transaction costs, especially at times when such networks are congested. Such a fee probably would become prohibitionist for those who intend to deal in small amounts of money.

Volatility: Because digital cryptocurrencies have a nature of extreme volatility, the losses in value that can happen almost at the break of the night are probably already one risk too large for people in poor regions where it is impractical to store or make day-to-day transactions with crypto.

6. Geographical and economic disparity

Crypto Accessibility: Developed vs. Developing Countries: In most developed countries, crypto is very accessible because a wide access to the internet is available in addition to established financial systems and light or clear regulatory frameworks. In developing nations, their people suffer with everything from infrastructure and stability to legality.

Crypto as an Inflation Hedge: People in countries with unstable currencies-for instance, Venezuela and Zimbabwe-flock to cryptocurrencies as an inflation hedge. Even then, it is highly dependent on good access to the Internet and the availability of crypto service facilities.

7. DeFi – Decentralized Finance

Access Without Banks: Probably one of the huge promises of DeFi is the possibility for users to be able to interact with financial services like lending, borrowing, and earning interest with no need for any bank interference. That could be quite a benefit, especially in jurisdictions with weak banking infrastructures.

Technical Issue: Most of the DeFi platforms are generally more complicated compared to centralized exchanges and require greater insight into the technologies used. This could be a real barrier for people whose technological knowledge background is weak and may dampen the possibility of their participation in DeFi.

8. Custodial versus Non-Custodial Wallets

Centralized/Custodial Wallets: The greater number of users approach the custodial wallets, whereby a given blockchain platform-say Coinbase and Binance-keeps your private key. Such solutions might be more seamless from a user experience perspective, or at least easier, for novices, but they require a certain amount of faith in a central organization.

non-custodial wallets are naturally decentralized, placing total control in the hands of a user through private keys, after which much more responsibility is expected from the user in securing the keys. In case it gets misplaced, there is no recovery for such a key or even ways to get it back, and this then presents a big drawback to users who are not so experienced.

9. Emerging Solutions to Improve Affordability

Layer 2 solutions are being developed to make transactions cheaper and further scale, including but not limited to Bitcoin's Lightning Network and Ethereum's Rollups, hence making crypto more usable in everyday life, while doing smaller purchases.

Stablecoins: These are USDT, USDC, or DAI-like stablecoins with an element of price stability by design, their valuation pegged on fiat money (1 to 1). Considering this, applying such tokens for transaction purposes will certainly be more reasonable in real life than highly volatile cryptocurrencies. Besides, stablecoins make DeFi more accessible for those users who rely on a stable store of value.

Mobile Wallets and Simplified Wallets: Companies all over the world are into the development of mobile applications to access their simplified wallet interfaces, which could make nontechnical users more familiar with cryptocurrency wallets and websites intended for exchanging purposes.

Conclusion:

In theory at least, Cryptocurrencies can practically be accessed by almost anybody. But then again, this sprouting potential for inclusiveness is actually tempered-by lack of access to the Internet, financial inclusion, regulatory barriers, and above all, transaction costs. In other words, though there is definitely a potential for inclusivity or financial empowerment, still, it is not available for all in practice. Only further improvement in technology, regulation, and education will be required for making crypto universally accessible.

21..What is a Crypto exchange?

Well, a cryptocurrency exchange is just an online place where one can buy, sell, and trade different cryptocurrencies. To make it even simpler, exchanges just act as means-intermediate services-between buyers and sellers, enabling users to trade cryptocurrency for other digital assets or just for fiat currencies, like the USD, EUR, or JPY. They come in two forms:

1. Centralized Exchanges (CEXs)
Centralized exchanges outsource the operation and management of exchanges to private companies. They usually provide seamless user experiences, high liquidity, and a number of trading pairs for the users. Popular examples of such centralized exchanges include:

- Coinbase: While the largest exchange based in the United States, it is highly user-friendly because it relies on following strict regulative policies.
- Binance: Has the largest trade volume of any exchange right now, lists a huge number of different cryptocurrencies, and trading pairs.
-Kraken is all about security, with a whole load of security features centered around the support of a wide variety of cryptocurrencies.

Key features for Centralized Exchanges include:

Order Books: Centralized exchanges have order books that perform the function of pairing the buying and selling orders. This means that the trading of users will be highly liquid and with the best price possible.

Custodial services store users' money. That means that the private keys to the crypto holdings of the users are kept with the exchange itself.
- Trading fees: These are charged by most, if not all, whenever some trade is done. In simple words, a maker and taker fee, deposit and withdrawal fee among others are included within this field of trade.
- Centralized exchanges: It offers customer support, more sophisticated trading utilities, and the ability to integrate other financial services.

Disadvantages:
- Centralized Control: Since the users' funds are kept in the exchange, this sets up one single failure point; hence, it's an attack point for hacking, fraud, or mismanagement.

- Regulatory Risk: Centralized exchanges need to adhere to their home rules and regulations and, therefore, may thus encounter a fair amount of inhibition or other juridical consequences depending on their domicile.

2. Decentralized Exchanges (DEXs)

These are contrasted by their decentralized counterparts, which are designed on smart contracts running over blockchain networks. They do not depend on an artificial ecosystem but are rather able to provide a capacity for trading directly among the users. A few examples of decentralized exchanges include:

-Uniswap: It is the most used Dex on Ethereum right now, even though the core functionality remains on an automated market-making model.

-SushiSwap is a decentralized exchange which came as a fork of Uniswap. They provide just the same functionality, and they bring in much more.

-PancakeSwap: The exchange in question is built on the Binance Smart Chain, offering low transaction fees and speedier trading.

Features of Decentralized Exchanges:

- Noncustodial: Users maintain complete custody of personal keys, therefore ultimately owning their money, minimizing most risks from hacking and misappropriation.

- Automated Market Makers: Most of the DEXs rely on AMMs for the aggregation of liquidity. This works by the mechanism where the user ends up trading against the pool and not an order book.

- Privacy and Anonymity: Most of these decentralized exchanges require very little, if any, information on an individual's identification, and on that note, grant one side more privacy than usual.

Disadvantages

Liquidity: Once traded, the liquidity pools of DEXs remain under development; hence, there is expected to be a difference in volume and price compared to what would be seen on a more liquid, centralized exchange.

The following are also disadvantages: - UX/UI: Not very user-friendly; advanced options for trading are highly limited.

Transactional charge: The Decentralized exchange via conventional ways will contain huge fluctuation in the fee, which might be higher with the burden or congestion of the Blockchain network.

Other normal features of digital or cryptocurrency exchanges include:

- Trading pairs: Those are the number of different pairs allowing the trading of one cryptocurrency for another or fiat currency in which all those exchanges are given.

- Order Variants: The exchange will give approval for various types of orders to be in place, such as market order, limit order, stop-loss order, among others.

Security features involved, are both in centralized and decentralized exchanges, that have taken all different measures to protect the funds of the user and his data by including 2FA, Encryption, and Cold Storage.

- User Interface: Most of the exchanges have interfaces to perform trading, balance enquiry, and account management. Centralized exchanges usually are fancier in their frontend when compared to decentralized exchanges.

Among many other contributors, cryptocurrency exchanges have grown incredibly in their contribution to the crypto ecosystem. They expose their users to a wide variety of different digital assets, each with its respective set of features, benefits, and associated risks.

22..What is DeFi (Decentralized Finance)?

DeFi in full means Decentralized Finance. DeFi is a class of digital assets and associated financial applications based on blockchain networks, notably Ethereum. It is all about rebuilding new financial systems and improving the prevailing ones by laying down protocols that are decentralized in nature, which would not require the need for some middlemen like banks or any other financial entities.

Key characteristics of DeFi:

1. Decentralized:
dApps, or DEFI applications, do keep running on some sort of decentralized network, typically a blockchain, kept by a set of nodes; in this case, there is no requirement for central governance or the utilization of any sort of intermediaries.

2. Smart Contracts:
These would also relate to DeFi because smart contracts are one sort of contract that executes themselves once the terms of agreement are written into lines of code. Smart contracts execute a transaction or probably the enforcement of an agreement based on some predefined conditions.

3. Transparency
Most DeFi protocols utilize open-source blockchains for recording most of the transactions and other operations. These events are done in full view, allowing any interested party to examine the code and, therefore, verify various types of transactions for free.

4. Interoperability:
Although most of the DeFi applications have been constructed based on Ethereum, they were

constructed to be compatible with other protocols of the same area. Therefore, interaction between these applications or other different services is easily maintainable.

5. Permissionless:
- It is open for anybody anywhere in the world, provided one has access to the internet. There is no middleman involved, meaning that clients of particular financial services need not go through institutions which traditionally were supposed to handle such services.

Some of the common DeFi applications are:

1. De-centralized Exchanges, aka DEXs:

Examples are Uniswap and SushiSwap.
The difference in operation is that in DEXes, buyers are able to trade in cryptocurrencies directly with another party without the use of any exchange. Trades are executed through automated market makers.

2. Borrowing and Lending

- Example: Aave, compound
These platforms give the possibility for users to lend their cryptocurrencies for some interest or to take some assets as a loan by collaterally putting money in. It's all managed through smart contracts.

3. Stablecoins:

Examples are DAI and USDC.
The subset of cryptocurrencies that keep the value stable relative to a certain fiat currency-for example, the U.S. dollar. Highly used in DeFi, really, for a stable medium and means of exchange, and even a store of value.

4. Yield farming and staking

Examples include: Yearn.finance, Curve Finance
The general underlying mechanism for yield farming in general involves the provision of liquidity to protocols of DeFi, where rewards are thereafter taken in, usually in the form of more tokens. The general definition of staking refers to the process of locking one's tokens in support of some network in return for a given reward.

5. Insurance:

Examples of this can be Nexus Mutual, Cover Protocol.

Insurance provided by DeFi insurance platforms covers hacks, problems relating to vulnerabilities in smart contracts, and any other issues in the DeFi ecosystem.

6. Derivatives and Synthetic Assets

Examples include: Synthetix, dYdX

A platform like this provides derivatives, which are financial instruments deriving values from an underlying asset-be it some cryptocurrencies, commodities, and/or securities. It allows one to hedge against or trade the value of such an asset in one form or another.

Advantages of DeFi:

-Accessibility: It reaches those people who have very limited to no access to banking.

- Low Cost: It saves or reduces a lot of costs that are associated with intermediaries or traditional financial services.

- Innovativeness: It avails an opportunity for new financial instruments, products, as well as services.

Risks and Challenges:

-Smart Contract Vulnerabilities: Bugs or exploits in these smart contracts could result in a loss of funds.

-Regulatory Uncertainty: Besides that, the current regulatory environment in which DeFi is allowed to work, while changing, could prove quite burdensome in the running and operation of DeFi platforms.

-Scalability: Most of the DeFi applications are facing challenges in terms of transaction speed and the fee required for making the transactions on Ethereum's network.

Conclusion:

DeFi represents the future of finance because, with the use of blockchain technology and smart contracts, it was meant to give decentralized, comprehensively clear, all-inclusive access to financial services. With as much enormous benefit and novelty as it brings into the space, risks and challenges are likewise presented that require users' caution.

23..What is a cryptocurrency wallet?
A cryptocurrency wallet is an online tool, to keep, manage, and trade on cryptocurrencies safely. In their most basic description, the following is what crypto wallets are and how they work:

Types of Crypto Wallets

1. Software Wallets
-Description: These are small computer applications or programs that can be downloaded hassle-free onto a computer or phone. They are more convenient for frequent usage but a bit more vulnerable online.

Types are:

- Desktop Wallets: Those which are set up on a desktop device. Examples include Exodus, Electrum.

- Mobile wallets: Examples of such mobile wallets, which are intelligent applications installed on your device, are Trust Wallet and Mycelium.

2. Hardware wallets
-Description: These are physical devices storing your cryptocurrency offline; thus, they offer the highest level of protection from hacking and malware. They are suitable for long-term storage. Examples include Ledger Nano S/X and Trezor One/ T.

3. Web Wallets
- Description: These wallets are web-based and usually provided by exchanges or online services. That is very convenient but requires one to trust the security of the provider.
Examples of these include MetaMask and the Coinbase Wallet.

4. Paper Wallets
-Cold storage: This is a physical printout or physical handwritten note containing the pairing of your public and private keys. Wholly offline but could get lost or damaged.
Paper Wallets -Examples: The physical, normally printed version of your wallet's Public and Private Keys in the form of QR codes.

5. Custodial Wallets
- Description: These are provided by the third-party services or exchanges. They will handle security and key management; this is convenient but places confidence in the custodian.

- Examples: Tezos wallets held on cryptocurrency exchanges like Binance or Kraken.

Key Factors

1. Public Key
- Receipt Crypto Address: This is a type of cryptographic key, utilized for the purposes of receiving cryptocurrencies, much like a digital address, to which others can send money. This is an alphanumeric string that can be copied and shared.

2. Private Key
- Description: A secret cryptographic key, utilized in transaction signing and access to one's cryptocurrency. A private key should not, whatsoever, be shown to anyone since the possession of a private key means possession of the funds.
It is an alphanumeric string that should always be kept secret and never given to others.

How Crypto Wallets Work:

1. Key Generation
- Description: When you create a new wallet, it generates a pair of cryptographic keys: a public key and a private key.

2. Key Storage
-Description: Wallets stores your private key safely. Hardware and paper wallets store keys offline.

3. Creating a transaction
- Explanation: Sending crypto means signing the transaction with your private key and letting the wallet broadcast over the blockchain network for inclusion in one of the blocks.

4. Collect Crypto
-It means that if a person is willing to send you cryptocurrency, you should at first share your public key or address with the sender, while the money in turn will fall in your wallet address and registered in blockchain.

Use Cases

1. Sending and Receiving a Cryptocurrency
Capability Description: Tracking the ability to send and receive various digital coins.

2. Storage of Cryptocurrency
 Secure your digital assets. A number of wallets offer either greater security or greater convenience.

3. Holdings tracking
- Description: It shows both the current balance and a list of transactions. Most wallets will enable some easy User Interface to track the state of one's asset portfolio.

4. Interacting with dApps
-Overview: So far, many wallets have been allowing one to connect in interaction with an ever-growing number of dApps and services, including DeFi and NFT markets.

Security Considerations

- Backup: Make regular backups of your wallet to avoid losing access. Most wallets have recovery phrases or seed phrases for this very reason.

- Safety of the Private Key: Never let your private key out; always make sure it is kept safe. Whosoever gets access to it shall be the sole controller of your funds.

- Two-Factor Authentication (2FA): Use 2FA where available to add an extra layer of security to your wallet.

One of the tools for digital management and transactions in cryptocurrencies is a crypto wallet, each available with different features, with differing levels of security, depending on your needs and use cases.

24..What is a crypto address?

A crypto address is a special identifier through which receipt and transmission of cryptocurrencies are done. Similar to an e-mail address or a bank account number, it is only in blockchain networks. The explanation of what a crypto address is and its uses will be described below:

1. Definition
-Crypto-address: Crypto-address shall mean an address of alphanumeric characters that have been derived from a public key. The crypto-address shall be considered the destination address utilized in receiving and sending any form of digital assets through virtual space.
Crypto address can be found in various combinations, but most of the time, it contains various combinations of alphabets and numbers in different manners.

2. The Types of Crypto Addresses
- Bitcoin (BTC): Bitcoin addresses in general will start with "1," "3," or "bc1" for the Bech32 format. Examples: `1A1zP1eP5QGefi2DMPTfTL5SLmv7DivfNa` and `bc1qar0srrr7xnxq4f5h02zqf3zv7u6r0pkztz8re` for a Bech32 address.
- Ethereum (ETH): Ethereum addresses are human-readable because they are prefixed by "0x" followed by 40 characters of the hexadecimal format. Example: `0x32Be343B94f860124dC4fEe278FDCBD38C102D88`.
- Litecoin (LTC): Litecoin addresses can start either with "L" or "M" and, respectively, can be in format quite similar to Bitcoin addresses: an example is `LcHhZkZbL1sFEx1HtuxDP7NB78TgjZBo3a`.

What will the crypto address be used for?

1. Receiving Cryptocurrency
-Details: You get cryptocurrency whenever you give the sender of the funds your crypto address; from there, he will use the address to send those funds into your wallet.
- Example: You are going to give a customer your Bitcoin address who would like to pay in BTC.

2. Sending Cryptocurrency

-Crypto Address: This address is what one would enter in his or her wallet once he or she wants to send some cryptocurrencies. Further, the address guides that money toward his or her account.
- Example: Sending Ethereum to your friend by entering your friend's Ethereum address in your wallet.

3. Transaction tracking
- Description: Crypto addresses can be used to track transaction history on the blockchain. The logic behind their use is that someone can input an address in some blockchain explorer and, therefore, show everything that relates to that address.
- Example: How to view the transaction history of your Bitcoin address on any Bitcoin block explorer.

4. Accuracy of Transactions
- Description: Crypto addresses play a major role in channeling funds to the proper destination. They prevent any kind of error in transaction routing.
Example: Always double-check the address of the person to whom one is sending something, lest one finds oneself in an argument when the funds have already been transferred to some other address altogether.

Security Considerations

1. Address Generation
Description: These are public keys run through a cryptographic algorithm to produce an address. Since each address would, therefore, be unique; when making a new address, a new key pair is generated in order to do so.
- Example: Each time a new wallet is generated, a new address for receiving funds is generated.

2. Address reuse
- Description: Address reuse is a form of leaking in privacy, given a situation where more than one transaction is involved with one address. Most of these transactions require the generation of an address anew.
Example: If every time one gets money, the address is generated newly, it goes a long way in ensuring privacy.

3. Address Verification
- Description: Make sure the address one is sending cryptocurrency to is correct, as once mined. Mistyped addresses or wrong addresses will lead to loss of funds.
Example: Copy-paste functions applied to the receiver's address verification reduces manual errors

Overview/Conclusion
A crypto address is the basic building blocks involved when dealing with cryptocurrencies. That would involve sending and receiving digital assets on a blockchain. Learning the use and management of crypto addresses therefore assure that cryptocurrencies will be managed in a secure and efficient manner.

25..Where and how to buy cryptos?

Invest in cryptocurrency in just a few simple steps: select a platform, create an account, and purchase your selected cryptocurrency. Following are the steps that explain comprehensively the ways through which you can purchase cryptocurrencies:

1. Choose the Cryptocurrency exchange or online trade website.

There are a few major kinds of platforms on which you can buy cryptocurrency. Of these, the most prevalent is exchanges for cryptocurrencies, though other options include P2P platforms, brokerage apps, and even ATMs.

Most Popular Virtual Currencies Exchanges:

Exchanges are websites that allow selling, buying, or trading in cryptocurrencies. Some of the known exchanges are:
- Coinbase: Great, intuitive interface for the beginner. The company is US-based.
- Binance: Again, this is available in a huge list of cryptocurrency options and at very low fees.
- Kraken is a US-based exchange that boasts of high security and a feature-rich marketplace.
- Gemini, which is heavily regulated and one of the more well-known exchanges in the United States.
- KuCoin has a long list of altcoin pairing with more advanced over-the-counter features.
- Bitstamp is probably the oldest of the exchanges in Europe, now one of the most trusted.

Brokerage Applications

Long story short, all of these platforms basically have the options to buy any kind of crypto, just like any other stock would be available, but most do not allow the withdrawal of crypto into a private wallet.

-Robinhood: This is an application used for buying and selling stocks; one can use it for buying cryptocurrency, too, though it does not support sending money into a wallet.
- PayPal and Venmo: Major purchasing, holding, and selling of crypto has been made possible on the biggest payment platforms, while functionality for crypto withdrawal has been limited or impossible in some cases.
-Peer-to-Peer (P2P) Platforms:
The P2P platforms enable one to buy cryptocurrencies directly from other persons. They link the seller and the buyer, hence acting as an intermediary between them.
-LocalBitcoins: This is a P2P website that allows you to purchase Bitcoin directly from individuals either in your vicinity or online.
Paxful: Another P2P, which enjoys huge support in a variety of pay means.

Cryptocurrency ATMs

You can also buy these cryptocurrencies from Bitcoin ATMs or any other cryptocurrency-dispensing ATM, actually. It is basically a kiosk at which you deposit some cash, and then you get the cryptocurrency directly into your wallet.

CoinATMRadar is now online to help anyone find Bitcoin or other cryptocurrency ATMs around them

2. Set Up an Account

After a proper selection of the platform is done; then, a person needs to get himself registered on that platform. The steps seem something like:

Account registration

- Provide an Email Address: Create an account first by providing your email and password.

It follows the generic pattern with some nuances: verification of a person's personality through the website or app-with photo ID, passport, driver's license, and maybe a selfie. You should expect it in the light of so-called "Know Your Customer" laws, which help to prevent fraud and money-laundering activities.

- Enable 2FA: enable two-factor authentication in your settings to add an additional layer of security to your account.

3. Deposit of funds

Before one invests in crypto, they have to deposit cash in the account. The payment methods differ from one exchange to another and according to one's country.

Means of Payments in Common Use

- Bank Transfer: Link the bank account and send the money across using ACH or SEPA. It usually has fewer fees, yet it takes about a few days.

-Credit or Debit Card: A number of these actually allow you to get instant crypto using your debit/credit card, but the fees may be a little higher at around 2-3%.

- Via PayPal: Very few of these online exchanges and P2P sites accept PayPal.

Fees for Depositing

The deposit fees also vary across different exchanges depending on the mode in which the funds are being deposited; bank transfers are usually cheap as opposed to credit and debit card payments.

4. Investment in Cryptocurrencies

You may simply purchase the cryptocurrency of your choice, given that your account is adequately funded.

How to Buy Crypto

- Cryptocurrency Choice: Choose the type of cryptocurrency you wish to buy. Example: Bitcoin, Ethereum, etc.

-Buy: You can place a market order where the execution of the order will be at the prevailing price of the crypto chosen coin, or you can place a limit order where you will have to state the price at which you want to buy.

- Confirm Transaction: Review the transaction information along with all the fees, then confirm your purchase.

Transaction Fees

Exchanges most often take their commission in one form or another-as a percentage of the purchase or sale made, ranging from 0.1 to 1.5%. Really, this depends on the particular platform one uses, be it market or limit order-type.

5. Store Your Cryptocurrency

After buying, one has to find out how he or she is going to store his or her cryptocurrency: leave it on the exchange or transfer it into a personal wallet for security reasons.

Types of Wallets:

* Hot wallets can be termed as online wallets since they are connected to the internet. This makes one in a position of easily and swiftly accessing them, but they are a bit fragile when it comes to being hacked.

- Trading Wallets: These are given out to you through an exchange you are on.

- Noncustodial wallets: Examples include Trust Wallet, MetaMask, or Coinbase Wallet.

* Cold Wallets: Hardware wallets are actual, physical devices that take on the appearance of a USB stick in appearance. They store crypto offline; therefore, much safer.

Ledger Nano S/X: Trezor is at the very top in the development of hardware cold wallets, which enable their user to carry a fat wallet full of cryptocurrencies.

6. Monitoring and management of your cryptocurrency

After buying a cryptocurrency, it's now time to follow up on the market or apply it as it shall fit.

- Holding: This means holding your cryptocurrency for an extended period and not selling it while keeping it for investment reasons.

- Trading: includes being actively involved in the buying and selling in cryptocurrency markets with a view to time the market action.

- Spending it: Use your cryptocurrency to buy anything from any of the merchants who accept it, perform peer-to-peer transactions, and use your crypto in general for anything related to decentralized finance.

Conclusion:

Worth noticing is that buying cryptocurrency presumes the choice of some platform, say Coinbase or Binance, creation of an account, depositing money, and buying crypto afterward. A little later, it will be great to transfer your crypto to a safe wallet. Mind the transaction fee and security of the exchange and wallet used.

It generally goes something like this in purchasing cryptocurrencies:

1. Choosing a Cryptocurrency Exchange:

Centralized Exchange: Examples include Coinbase, Binance, and Kraken. They actually possess an extremely friendly interface, with very good liquidity.

Decentralized Exchange: Examples include Uniswap, SushiSwap, and PancakeSwap. They have no sort of governing authority in their core and seem to always use a wallet.

2. Create an Account

-Registration: After that, when the right exchange is selected, it asks to input an e-mail and a password.

-Verify Identity: Give verification of identity by stating the information needed and attaching identification documents and proof of residence where applicable.

3. Lock Down Your Account
- Activating two-factor authentication (2FA): This will add an additional layer of security, whereby access to user information and other essential data can only be granted after authenticating with an additional security measure.

- Password Strength: Minimum incomparable strength of password is required at the time of sign-up.

4. Deposit Funds
Bank Transfer or Credit/Debit Card: Most of them would give you an option to deposit fiat currency through bank transfers by credit or debit card.

- Crypto deposit: Fund an exchange account with a cryptocurrency transfer, provided one already has some cryptocurrency.

5. Request an Order
- Cryptocurrency to Be Purchased: Many exchanges would provide a drop-down menu of the cryptocurrencies on sale in their inventory.

Type of order selected:
- Market Order: This is an order to buy at the current market price.
- Limit Order: When the order needs to be placed for a certain quantity at an exact price, it will be executed when the market will reach that very price.
- Amount: Choose the amount of cryptocurrency you want to buy, or the amount of fiat currency you would like to spend.

6. Make the Payment
- Review and Confirm: A thorough scrutiny of the details of your order, along with all the associated fees, will be presented for your confirmation.

- Confirm the transaction: Finally, this will credit your cryptocurrency into your account on the exchange.

7. Withdraw to a Wallet "Optional but Recommended"
Here are some considerations: Choose a wallet: To supplement the security concerns, consider moving your cryptocurrency off the exchange into a personal wallet, be it software or hardware.

- Initiate Withdrawal: Open the exchange's withdrawal section, fill in your wallet address, and confirm the transaction. Be extra careful with the address, because one tiny mistake means your funds are in a black hole.

8. Monitor and Control
- Price Tracking: Keep track of the value of your cryptocurrency with some specific exchange or wallet apps.

- Keep Informed: Follow all current news and development updates in the markets regarding cryptocurrency.

Additional Hints:

- Research: Know what cryptocurrency you are buying and the project behind the creation.

- Fees: How much is one charged to transact with sometimes called withdrawal fee by the exchange.

-Legal conditions: Buy and trade cryptocurrency, which needs to be legally permitted in your location.

These are the easy steps by which one can buy some cryptocurrencies in a secure and efficient manner and go another step further in this digital asset market.

26..Where and how to store cryptos?

Safekeeping of the cryptocurrency is important in protecting one's wealth against theft, loss, and unauthorized access. Several techniques and utilities can be used for crypto storage, each offering its own merits regarding security and convenience. Below is a brief overview of major ways:

1. **Software Wallets**

- Desktop Wallets:
 Examples: Exodus, Electrum

Local installs to your computer: These represent a decent compromise between convenience and security; however, for as long as the computer is compromised, they equally could be vulnerable to malware infection or being hacked.

- Mobile Wallets:
Examples of such wallets include Trust Wallet, Coinomi.

A mobile wallet is essentially an application for smartphones; it offers the same conveniences in every instance of daily life and transaction. This exchange may be rather less secure compared to hardware wallets, yet it's good for ease of access.

- Web Wallets:
 Examples: Metamask, Coinbase Wallet

Web wallets accessed from a web browser. Most of the exchanges offer web wallets. They are probably the easiest to use and one of the most exposed to compromise because private keys have to be exposed to access.

2. **Hardware Wallets**
Examples include Ledger Nano S/X and Trezor One/Model T.

Hardware wallets are physical mediums that store your private keys offline using the most secure modes. Being extremely resistant to hacking and malware attacks, they throw greater responsibility at you for keeping the device safe and secure.

3. <u>Paper Wallets</u>
Examples: Generated by web service like "Bitaddress.org".

The paper wallet entails printing out the private and public keys on a paper base; storage is thereafter done in some safe location. Though offline and hence not subject to digital attacks, it can easily get lost and damaged. They require very good handling and storage.

4. <u>Custodial Wallets</u>
Some of them are provided by exchanges like "Binance" and "Coinbase".

Those involving custodial wallets are driven by third parties, such as cryptocurrency exchanges. Among the advantages involved in the use of a custodial wallet is how easy it can be in use. Security measures are all that determines their safety since the private keys that a user is in possession of do not have control.

<u>There are many best practices for the storage of cryptocurrencies.</u>

1. Mix it up
Combining more methods used for storage, therefore, makes security better; for instance, a hardware wallet may be appropriate for long-term storage, and, another wallet form may be appropriate for everyday transactions, such as mobile or desktop wallet.

2. Backups:
-Back up your private key/seed recovery phrases in your wallet regularly and store them safely in more than one place. Then, in case it's somehow lost or damaged, you can recover your asset.

3. Private Key Generation
- Never share private keys or recovery phrases with anyone. Store them offline and in an extremely safe place, like in a safe or a secure document storage facility.

4. Enable Two-Factor Authentication (2FA):
- Use 2-factor authentication on any platform or wallet that provides such functionality, because this gives a basic level of extra security to protect your account.

5. Keep watch out for Phishing:
-Be aware of a phishing attempt and know whether you are at the right place or at an application where you should enter your sensitive information.

6. Follow up very frequently.

-This will involve frequent software and firmware updates so as to ensure users get recent developments made, in addition to more security patches that have been made.

Conclusion: The best kind of storage for cryptocurrency depends upon one's needs and security level required. "Hardware wallets" offer the highest level of security for long-term storage, while "software wallets" provide convenience for regular use. Paper wallets are secure but in offline mode and require very careful handling. "Custodial wallets" offer ease of use but depend on the security of the provider. Always follow the best practices to safeguard your assets.

27..Hot and cold cryptos storage:

'cold storage' or 'hot storage' are 2 different aspects of storing digital assets.

Both terms are defined hereunder:

1.Cold Storage: Cold Storage is a term that defines the fact of holding currencies offline. By this are meant assets which, do not have access to the internet, and kept guarded against hacking malware.

- Types of Cold Storage: - Hardware Wallets: These are devices to which private keys are usually put offline. The examples include Ledger Nano S/X and Trezor. They only connect to a computer when the user needs them, thus offering a very secure defense against online attacks.

Paper wallets, or even hand-written notes, are papers that contain your private keys and public addresses. These are totally offline but should be kept in safety, safe from any form of physical damage or loss.

Air-Gapped Computers: That is just a computer that has never been connected to the internet. This computer is used for creating and storing private keys offline, and even for signing up transactions in a secure way.

- Advantages:

- Safety: That option can't be hacked, phished, or even forced to download malware because it is operating offline.

- Long-term storage: Useful for storing large quantities of cryptocurrency that you do not intend to use immediately.

- Drawbacks: Inconvenience: The assets held in cold storage are not very convenient as only a physical form of access is allowed, either from the storage device itself or even from a paper wallet. However, there is another risk, which is:
- Physical Risk: Your cold storage, or paper wallet for instance or even a hardware wallet, is at risk of getting lost, stolen, or even destroyed.

2**. Hot Storage**: Hot storage refers to the storage of cryptocurrency assets online, that is, on the internet. Those assets are meant to be used very frequently or even day to day. There are primarily two kinds of Hot Storage:

- Software Wallets: Apps or software that keep the private key in the computer or mobile device. Some of the examples include; Exodus, Electrum, and Trust wallet. They are very convenient for constant use but more vulnerable to threats that start online. And then there is another type: exchange wallets. Those are wallets made available by an exchange to a user in order to store his funds with the view to trading.

Examples are wallets on the Coinbase or Binance platform. Although easy to access, it may be very vulnerable to the risks associated with an exchange.

-Web Wallets: This is an account service storing the private keys on the server side, so users can retrieve them using their web browser. Examples include MetaMask and MyEtherWallet. They are convenient, but can be at risk, in an online attack

Some advantages:

Convenience: Access and use for more convenient transactions and trading are easier and faster.

Liquidity: Any periodic management or access to assets and/or trading based on periodic frequencies.

Disadvantages: It is at a great risk of hacking, phishing, and malware because it is always connected to the internet. Custodial Risks: In the case of exchange and web wallets, the risk is that the service provider is compromised or goes offline.

Best Practices: Hybrid Approach: Most of the users combine both kinds of approaches whereby cold storage is used for long-term holdings and hot storage for active funds.

Back Up private keys and recovery phrases for both mechanisms. Hot and cold storage to be regularly backed up in case of loss or damage.

Security: The wallet should be secure; the 2-factor authentications, encryption for all transfers, and room for physical storage of the cold storage device must be in place.

Conclusion: Cold storage is the safest way to secure cryptocurrency from every online threat. It's basically designed for long-term storage. Hot storage gives convenience and access for higher risks. Everything depends on a mix of both techniques based on your needs and security preferences for an effective management strategy in cryptocurrency.

28..Is it risky?
Crypto investment is fundamentally a very risky affair. Though several people have earned big through this, on the other hand, the market is extremely speculative and volatile. Whether it is a change of regulations, some technological hitches, or for that matter some change in sentiment, extreme volatility may happen at any time. Proper research regarding the same should, therefore, be done and the risks considered prior to making a plunge. Diversification and putting in only that amount which one can afford to lose would thus be the prudent criteria.

29..Can it be stolen?
Yes, your crypto coins can actually get stolen from your wallet if your security practices are not good enough. The most frequent methods of such theft are as follows:

1. Phishing: When a person is tricked into disclosing his private keys by masquerading as a website, telephone, or other way of communication, and asks for logging on with his information.

2. Malware: Some malware was designed to access either your wallet or your private keys.

3. Scams: Schemes that will finally hoodwink you and have you revealed your private information in order to transfer your coins.

4. Hacking: An attack directly on the Crypto exchanges and low-security wallets.
Employ strong passwords, enable 2FA, secure your private keys, and avoid suspicious links or requests to avoid losing your assets. Consider the use of a hardware wallet for added security.

30..What is a Bitcoin ETF?

One of the financial instruments that will ensure exposure to the price of Bitcoin is a Bitcoin ETF, whereby an investor is assured that he is exposed to the price of Bitcoin without being actually required to buy, hold, and manage the cryptocurrency himself. Major issues that surround Bitcoin ETFs revolve around the following:

1. What is a Bitcoin ETF?
- Structure: A Bitcoin ETF is generally an investment fund trading on conventional stock exchanges just like the trade of regular stocks. Commonly, the value of such a fund is pegged to the price of Bitcoin, hence mirroring Bitcoin's performance.
- Underlying Asset: The actual Bitcoin that the fund holds, or it can be valued using futures and other derivatives pegged to the price of Bitcoin.
- Trading: The shares of the ETF can be bought or sold at any instant of trading in the stock exchanges, just like any other publicly traded stock or ETF.

2. Types of Bitcoin ETFs
- Physical Bitcoin ETFs store the actual Bitcoin in custodial accounts. Ownership of the underlying Bitcoin is represented with shares of the ETF. This represents the most direct way to be exposed to Bitcoin but is less common due to regulatory hurdles.
Those that are futures-based belong to this category. The futures-based ETF is that particular kind of ETF that normally invests in Bitcoin futures contracts and actually not in Bitcoin. Bitcoin futures are an agreement to sell or buy Bitcoin at a specified time in the future at an already determined price. In reality, futures-based ETFs allow for indirect exposure to the prices of Bitcoin, where allowed, and tend to happen more in large markets like the United States.

3. Purposes of the Bitcoin ETF:
-Access: With Bitcoin ETFs, mainstream investors would most likely join the market, without going through all those hassles of cryptocurrency exchanges, fiddling with private keys, and dealing with the intricacies of a digital wallet.
- Regulatory Compliance: Although all the ETFs are financial products that come under governance by regulation, investment in the Bitcoin ETF offers a form of regulatory overview/ investor protection not presented during direct crypto trades across unregulated platforms.
- Portfolio Diversification: Investors also invest in their portfolios through the avenue of Bitcoin ETFs, just as would be done for any other ETF on stocks or bonds. It actually provides one with a painless avenue of diversification into cryptocurrency markets.
- Tax Efficiency: Generally, ETFs are viewed as tax-efficient investment vehicles. Owning an ETF of Bitcoin would hugely simplify the tax implications of one's investment in Bitcoin, rather than the capital gains taxes levied from direct transactions in Bitcoins.
- Liquidity: Since the Bitcoin ETFs would be listed on the biggest of stock exchanges, this amounts to liquidity, where every investor can sell or buy his or her shares at any time during market hours.

4. The advantages of a Bitcoin ETF:
- No Crypto Wallet Headaches: Investors will not have to worry about how to store and safely keep their Bitcoin.
-Traditional Investment Accounts: Investors will also be free to purchase the Bitcoin ETF using normal brokerage accounts-meaning that even more and more people can be allowed to participate, including even those retired accounts such as IRAs.
- Familiarity: To investors who are more accustomed with traditional financial products, a Bitcoin ETF represents a conduit to investment in Bitcoin without necessarily going into the crypto space.

5. Risk and Consideration:
- Price tracking: Some ETFs-especially the ones based on futures-may have a price tracking problem in relation to the spot price of Bitcoin, simply because of the nature of futures contracts and the cost of their rollover.
- Management Fees: Bitcoin ETFs charge management fees, which eat into the returns compared with any direct investment in Bitcoins.
- Market Risks: As with all investments, there is a certain amount of market risk involved, and Bitcoin exchange-traded funds are no different. Bitcoin as an asset class is extremely volatile, and this volatility would also reflect in the pricing of the fund.
- Regulatory Risks: The regulatory environment for Bitcoin and cryptocurrency ETFs is still changing and could affect the availability and composition of these products.

6. Examples of Bitcoin-ETFs include:
ProShares Bitcoin Strategy ETF: It is a fund tracking bitcoin with CME-traded futures contracts. Technically, this is an ETF related to bitcoin, not directly, but as a bitcoin future-based ETF. It is listed on the NYSE. It has been the first ETF related to bitcoin to get the United States' Security and Exchange Commission's approval.
Purpose Bitcoin ETF-BTCC: The world's first physically-settled Bitcoin ETF, which was initiated in Canada, is holding the cryptocurrency outright. It was listed and trades on the Toronto Stock Exchange.

In Short:
A Bitcoin ETF is a means through which one can get exposure to Bitcoin without the hassles of buying and managing the cryptocurrency. It has been used primarily for investment purposes, offering a regulated, easily accessible, and simplified route to invest in Bitcoin through traditional financial markets. Like all investments, Bitcoin ETFs also carry their own set of risks and considerations.
So far, many cryptocurrency ETFs have been launched to the market, offering a range of ways in which investors can dive into cryptocurrencies. Here are some of the major crypto ETFs in existence:

1. Bitcoin ETFs

- ProShares Bitcoin Strategy ETF (BITO):
Type: Tracking futures Bitcoin ETF
- Description: The BITO is the very first Bitcoin ETF to be given green lit status by the U.S. Securities and Exchange Commission, finding its inception in October 2021. It doesn't invest directly into the asset Bitcoin but instead follows an investment strategy in Bitcoin Futures.

• Valkyrie Bitcoin Strategy ETF, BTF
Type: Bitcoin ETF based on futures

- Description: The second of several Bitcoin ETFs that would release further into the future, much like BITO, only it is later. It provides targeted exposure to the Bitcoin futures trading on the Chicago Mercantile Exchange, or CME.

- VanEck Bitcoin Strategy ETF: XBTF
- Type: Bitcoin ETF based on futures
- Description: This also invests in Bitcoin futures but is being managed by the super well-acknowledged investment management company known as VanEck.

- Purpose Bitcoin ETF (BTCC):
- Type: Physical Bitcoin ETF
- Description: BTCC is the world's first physically settled Bitcoin ETF that directly holds Bitcoin and is listed on the Toronto Stock Exchange.

Evolve Bitcoin ETF - EBIT
- Type: Physical Bitcoin ETF
- Description: EBIT is another physically settled Bitcoin ETF that is traded on TSX, granting investors direct exposure to Bitcoin.

- CI Galaxy Bitcoin ETF (BTCX):
- Product Type: Physical Bitcoin ETF
- Description: BTCX invests directly in the cryptocurrency bitcoin, in an attempt to replicate the underlying asset performance, less any fees. Listed and trading on the TSX.

2. Ethereum-based ETFs

- Purpose Ethereum ETF (ETHH):
- Type: Physically Settled Ether ETF
- Description: ETHH aims to provide investors with direct exposure to Ethereum, listed on TSX.

Evolve Ethereum ETF (ETHR):
Product Type: Physical Ethereum ETF
- Description: An ETF that tracks Ethereum, which is an available investment for investors, trading on the TSX.

- CI Galaxy Ethereum ETF ETHX -
- Type: Physical Ethereum ETF
-Description: Incepted in March 2021, ETHX is designed to provide pure exposure to Ethereum. It is listed on the TSX.

3. Multi-Crypto ETFs

- Bitwise 10 Crypto Index Fund (BITW)
- Type: Multi-Crypto Fund
-Description: The investment seeks to track the Bitwise 10 Large Cap Crypto Index, made up of the two largest cryptocurrencies, namely Bitcoin and Ethereum, among others. Yet, the result was that it got listed on the OTCQX market.

- Galaxy Crypto Index Fund BRPHF:
- Type: Multi-Crypto Fund
- Description: This fund, managed by Galaxy Digital, aims to provide exposure to a diversified portfolio of cryptocurrencies. It is listed on the OTCQX market.

4. Other notable Crypto ETF:
- Amplify Transformational Data Sharing ETF (BLOK):
- Type: Blockchain Technology ETF
Description: Although this is not a direct crypto ETF, it's actually an investment in those firms that deal in blockchain technology and even crypto assets. A good indirect exposure to the cryptocurrency market, BLOK offers investors an opportunity in the crypto space.

- Global X Blockchain ETF (BKCH):
- Type: Blockchain Technology ETF
- Description: The ETF is designed to track the innovation economy, but includes several blockchain-related technologies and digital assets that would provide indirect exposure to the crypto industry.

Conclusion
The crypto ETF market has broadly expanded one's access, both directly and indirectly, into cryptocurrencies. Bitcoin and Ethereum ETFs would be a direct exposure to the two leading cryptocurrencies, while multi-crypto and blockchain ETFs would provide diversified or thematic exposure to the general crypto ecosystem. Be that as it may, the market is bound to further evolve, and new products and options no doubt will crop up.

31..How to send and receive cryptocurrencies?
Send and receive cryptocurrency with the help of a digital wallet, which will store your private and public keys and allow interaction with different blockchain networks. Now, let's explain how to perform both in detail:

1. Setting Up a Wallet:
Choose a Wallet Type:
- Software Wallets: This might refer to an application downloaded, maybe installed on a computer or mobile device. Examples include MetaMask, Trust Wallet, and Exodus.

- Hardware wallets refer to the actual devices themselves that private keys can be kept on offline, with very high security, such as Ledger and Trezor.

- Hot Wallets / exchange wallets are online wallets hosted by exchanges themselves, like Binance, Coinbase, and Kraken. They are super convenient and straightforward to use, but somewhat less secure than self-controlled wallets, since the exchange retains the custody of the private key.

- Paper Wallets: These are a printed version of any key pairings of your public and private keys. As they are seldom used these days, this too could be a form of cold storage.

First, let's make a wallet.
First, download wallet software and install it, or simply create an account if one is using an exchange

wallet.

This in essence is the general following of installation instructions, setting up a strong password, and backing up of your wallet's recovery seed phrase, which is a series of words able to restore access to your wallet.

2. Receiving crypto:

- Copy your wallet address:

Open your Wallet application and find your receive address; it can usually be found under "Receive" or "Deposit."

- The address will be a very long string of alphanumeric and will most probably be represented in the form of a QR code.

- Relinquish your address:

You are supposed to give this address to whoever will send the cryptocurrency. You should confirm and reconfirm because, if wrong, the transaction can never be reverted nor returned to the owner.

- Confirm the transaction:

The sender will do the transaction; then after several minutes or even one hour, depending on how fast the blockchain network is, you will see the income of cryptocurrency in your wallet.

Most of them will notify you upon the confirmation of a transaction, and the amount will show in your wallet.

3. Sending Crypto:

Recipient address:

Get the recipient's wallet address from whom you will be exchanging your digital currency. Make sure this address is accurate, and you have double-checked with the owner that it is the correct one for the correct blockchain-for example, not sending Bitcoin on an Ethereum address.

- Enter Details of Transaction:

Open your wallet and go to the "Send" or "Withdraw" section.

Follow through by filling in the box with the recipient's address and the quantity of cryptocurrency you want to send.

Some wallets will allow you to set the transaction fee; the fee determines the speed at which the transaction is processed. Thus, the higher the fee, the faster the confirmation.

- Review and Confirm:

Check all of the information, but particularly the recipient's address and the amount.

Confirm the transaction. At this point, the transaction is broadcast on the network and cannot be recovered.

- Transaction Confirmation:

It may take some minutes to even hours depending on the flow of transactions on the network before it gets full confirmation that indeed the recipient has the money in his account.

A TXID (Transaction ID) provided by your wallet, can be used to track further information about the transaction status on any blockchain explorer.

4. Security Best Practices:
- Use Secure Wallets: Always choose reputable wallets and keep your software up to date.
- Protect Private Keys and Seed Phrase: Never let another person access the private key or recovery seed phrase of your wallet, but rather store them in some offline and secure form.
- Provide a correct address: ensure that the address is scanned properly and correctly before sending the funds. Because funds which have been lost due to mistake of address will never be recovered.
- Enable 2FA: Two-step authentication will be helpful, so, if at all possible, enable it to bring ultimate security either to your wallet or exchange account.

Conclusion:
In this respect, cryptocurrency sending and receiving is an easy task, but shall be handled with care. Indeed, keeping cryptocurrency transactions safe while operating them is an easy thing to handle with a safe wallet and good habits.

32..What are gas fees?
Any amount that one pays for participating in any transaction or execution of smart contracts in any cryptocurrency network is the gas fee. Using the example of the Ethereum network, the gas fees basically go as a reward to miners who validate and record the transactions on the blockchain. The amount charged as a fee is sometimes determined by how congested the network is, including the complication of the transaction. High demand mostly translates to high gas fees because many users compete for faster processing of transactions.

33..How many cryptos are at the market today?
Currently, more than 24,000 cryptocurrencies, up until August 2024, have been listed on different platforms and databases. It is something that does not stop, since new projects enter the scene, while others turn inactive or are delisted.
Of the thousands of digital coins out there, by far the majority remain rather obscure; just a few of them have gained remarkable market attention and traction so far. The biggest ones, such as Bitcoin and Ethereum, are the most well-known and in wide use, while many others have more niche applications or serve a particular purpose in their respective blockchains.

34..What are the cryptos different types?
Cryptocurrencies, based on their main uses and the kind of technology put in place, can be divided into:

1. **Coins**
- Description: Originally, a coin would refer to any cryptocurrency that exists independently, and on their blockchain. Most of them are developed to be utilized as some form of digital cash or as a store of value.
- Examples
Bitcoin can be seen as some form of digital gold to be used as a store of value.
Ethereum: Although it also serves as an exchange medium, like BTC, its overall popularity is mainly in smart contracting.

2. Tokens
Tokenization is the creation, through smart contracts, of tokens on preexisting blockchains, representative of any given asset or right.
- Types:

* Utility tokens: are those providing the buyer access to some sort of product or service in an ecosystem.
UNI on Uniswap: This token became adopted in all respects for governance and participation-related processes across its Uniswap decentralized exchange.

* Security Token: Represent the ownership of some form of underlying asset or company, therefore making them subjects to regulatory control.
Example: Polymath (POLY) allows users to issue security tokens.

3. Stablecoin
- Description: They are designed to peg their value to one big fiat currency or to another asset, so as to reduce the bug of volatility.

Examples include
- USDT Tether: A cryptocurrency created specifically always to be at par in value with the US dollar.
- USD Coin (USDC): Pinned to the US dollar, too.
- DAI: A decentralized stablecoin that is pegged to the US dollar.

4. Privacy Coins
- Description: this type of coins improve privacy and anonymity of the transactions, and make tracing really difficult as to who the sender and recipient are, and the amount of transaction involved.
Examples include
- Monero (XMR): Ring signature and stealth address are introduced to implementation related to privacy.
-Zcash: This cryptocurrency is completely dependent on zero-knowledge proof in order for the list of transactions, in terms of confidentiality, to be full.

5. Platform Tokens
- Description: The described below will be utilized as native coins within those platforms which provide an environment to build decentralized applications and smart contracts.
- Examples
- Ethereum, ETH: Provided when paying the transactions of deploying and executing codes atop the Ethereum platform.
- Cardano, ADA: It is a coin required to incentivize a participant in order to make use of the Cardano network and Cardano's smart contract ecosystem.

6. Governance Tokens
Description: A token holder would have a right to vote and would also contribute on how a certain project or protocol will operate at a decentralized level.
Examples include:

Compound (COMP): This token is used for governance over the Compound DeFi platform.
AAVE - This is used in governance for the Aave Lending Protocol.

7. Wrapped Tokens
It describes the ability of other blockchains to represent assets belonging to one blockchain in realizing the interoperability between any two blockchains.
Examples:
WBTC: Wrapped Bitcoin: This stands for the wrapped form of Bitcoin, its representation lying on the Ethereum Blockchain.
WETH - Wrapped Ether: Wrapped Ether to interact with Open-source DApp DEX built on the Ethereum Blockchain; open-source code.

8. Forked Coins
- Description: A new digital currency born out of the fork of an already existing cryptocurrency blockchain. Forks can be "hard" with the creation of a new blockchain or "soft" by updating the already existing blockchain.
- Examples:
Bitcoin Cash BCH: Bitcoin went into fork in 2017; with increased block size.

Litecoin (LTC): that is, also a cryptocurrency forked from Bitcoin back in the year 2011, though they have several sorts of technical changes.

9. Meme Coins
- Meme : Mainly a creation, but most of the time an inside joke, passed through virtual communities and social networks.
- Example:
DOGE - Dogecoin: This began as a joke, but has grown impressively and now have a very real-world use.

Each coin has a different purpose, and all differ in various ecosystems, adding a fillip to diversity and functionality in the crypto space.

35..Difference between crypto coins and types.

They could be divided into many types regarding technology, function, or purpose. Understanding the differences between such types will probably ease your way into the crypto world. Now, allow me to present to you some basic differences between crypto coins and the major categories of cryptocurrencies.

1.Coins vs Tokens
Arguably, the most basic differentiation within the world of cryptocurrency is the one between "coins" and "tokens."

* Coins.
-Definition: Coins are the cryptocurrencies operating on their blockchain. In most cases, coins have been employed as mediums of exchange or stores of value within their network.

- Purpose: Most coin uses are transactional in nature-that is, a medium of transferring value-with only very few exceptions in governance, or staking, on their respective blockchains.
Examples
- Bitcoin (BTC): The first cryptocurrency is mainly a store of value, or being used for person-to-person direct payments.
- Ethereum (ETH): A blockchain designed for smart contract execution, for decentralizing applications, but the coin, Ether, nonetheless has to be used for paying the transaction fees.
- Litecoin (LTC): an even lighter, speedier version of Bitcoin, meant for the commoner forms of transactions.

*Tokens
Tokens are cryptocurrency assets built on top of previously developed blockchains, typically Ethereum or other similar smart-contract cryptographic currencies. They do not have a blockchain of their own but depend on some blockchain they have been issued on.
- Purpose: Tokens can represent various types of assets, and numerous different purposes. Common applications are dApps, governance, utility, and sometimes even an ecosystem in general.

Examples:
- ERC-20 Tokens: They were issued on the Ethereum network. Examples include but are not limited to Uniswap-UNI, Chainlink-LINK, and USD Coin-USDC.
- BEP-20 Tokens Natively built on the Binance Smart Chain, these include PancakeSwap (CAKE) and Binance USD (BUSD).
- NFTs or non-fungible token, are a representative of a unique digital asset, where each of them acts like a title of ownership for an item, artwork, or other forms of assets. They become quite common in gaming and art environments.

2. Types of Cryptocurrencies:
Depending on how one might want to classify them-based on their application, technology, or platform-there are various types of available cryptocurrencies with several categories. Some of the main types include:

a. Cryptocurrencies for payment uses
In a nutshell:
- Purpose: Intended to be used for transactions, as an alternative form of digital cash, just like fiat currencies such as the USD, EUR, and others.
Examples :
- Bitcoin: This was the very first cryptocurrency and is a lot more comparable to digital gold, being able to be used as a store of value.
- Litecoin (LTC): Emerged as a fast alternative that is twice as speedy for fast transactions, less expensive than BTC for everyday transactions.
- BCH: it is an abbreviation for Bitcoin Cash and is actually just a fork of Bitcoin. So, it does bear large block sizes that are capable of executing faster transaction times.

b. Stablecoin
Stable coins are tokens having relatively stable values that are pegged to the value of a fiat currency, whether USD, EUR, or any such currency, or even baskets of assets. They thereby reduce volatility associated with most traditional crypto coins.
Fiat-backed, or fiat collateralized: Fully collateralized 1:1 by reserves of some sort of fiat currency, often US dollars. Examples:
- USDT, a currency that is pegged against the U.S. dollar.
- USD Coin (USDC): It is dollar pegged and, like the others, a reserve-backed one as well.
- Crypto-collateralized: This means it is collateralized by other cryptocurrencies; however, it is over-collateralized enough to take into consideration its volatility.
- DAI: It is an algorithmic stablecoin and comes on the Ethereum blockchain for asset issuance. It's an algorithmic stablecoin whose algorithms and smart contracts ensure that its pegging remains intact, and it does not have an underlying asset.
- Then there is also TerraUSD, or UST for short-the example of an algorithmic stablecoin-though its dramatic collapse in 2022 highlighted several risks with such models.

c. Utility Tokens
- Function: Utility tokens are used to access services or functions in a defined blockchain. They tend to carry value since they are needful to use in certain applications.
- Examples:
- ETH technically is a coin; however, the entity is more of a utility token in which one uses in order to pay the gas within the Ethereum ecosystem.
- Chainlink: It was designed for use in the Chainlink decentralized oracle network.
- Filecoin: FIL is a token usable for access to decentralized storage offered on the Filecoin network.

d. Governance Tokens
 - Purpose : These tokens are there for the holders; therefore, to empower the distribution of the vote power in decentralized protocols. Governance tokens gives the right to the users to take part in decision-making, like to make protocol updates or changes.
- Examples:
- Uniswap (UNI): All of the tokens issued, enjoyed the right to propose and vote on changes to the Uniswap decentralized exchange protocol.
- Maker (MKR): This is one of the tokens that govern MakerDAO, a decentralized lending protocol.
- AAVE: the change and improvement proposal of the protocol are put to vote to its owners in the Aave DeFi system.

e. Private Coins
Purposes: Anonymity. Privacy coins can facilitate anonymous transactions. Nobody has managed to beat their security so far compared to general cryptographic practice. They use sophisticated methods which can even obscure information about the transaction and the parties.
- Examples:
Privcoin, but rebranded itself as Monero - XMR, probably one of the most known coins when it comes to privacy, with a focus on untraceable transactions.

Zcash (ZEC): Any transaction can be shielded or transparent in order to provide the highest level of anonymity for users.

DASH (DASH): It is a digital currency that has an in-built optional feature of Private Send available for the users.

f. Decentralized Finance (DeFi) Coins

- Application: DeFi coins, are applied in lending, borrowing, trading, and even earning interest through decentralized financial protocols. The idea really goes towards the introduction of decentralized equivalents to the existing traditional financial systems which may include banks, loans, exchanges, etc. using the decentralized blockchain technology.

Examples:

- AAVE: Aave is a token that operates on the Aave lending and borrowing protocol.

- Compound is a governance token for the Compound Lending Protocol.

- SNX Synthetics were synthesized through a synthesis process, are crypto-backed derivatives, and could be issued on the Synthetix protocol.

g. NFTs: Nonfungible tokens

Purpose: The NFT represents ownership of a specific digital asset, which can be a piece of art, music, virtual land, or an in-game item-whatever it is, unique and not interchangeable with another cryptocurrency on a 1:1 basis.

Examples:

- CryptoPunks are among the first and best-developed collections in the history of NFTs.

- Bored Ape Yacht Club: Actually, one of the most traded NFT collections. This is always traded for a very expensive price.

-Axie Infinity (AXS), play-to-earn game that had given users a collection of NFTs to use in the game.

h. CBDCs or Central bank digital currencies

- Purpose: CBDCs are issued by the central bank as a digital version of a national fiat currency. They are, however, not the same thing as traditional cryptocurrencies, but, are based on blockchain or other forms of digital ledger technologies.

Examples:

- e-CNY, or Digital Yuan, is a digital currency issued by the Central Bank of China.

- Digital Euro: The European Central Bank is exploring a digital version of the euro.

- Bahama Sand Dollar: This is one of the earliest CBDCs, and was designed by the Central Bank of the Bahamas.

3. **The difference between different types of crypto coin**

Functionality:

- Payment Coins. These are coins, and generally, they are used in transactions. Examples include Bitcoin and Litecoin.

- Utility Tokens: give access to use a product or service in return; for instance, Ethereum or Chainlink.

- Stable coins: Used for its lower volatility and stabilization of the average transaction: one that handles every-day transactions. Some examples are Tether and USDC.

-Governance Tokens: These entitle the owner to vote on and participate in the decisions related to such decentralized projects as could be best represented by Uniswap and Aave.

- Privacy Coins: These coins focus much attention on the anonymity and the private nature of the transaction (Monero, Zcash).

Blockchain Base

-Coins: In their absolute forms operate on their own Blockchains; Examples include Bitcoin and Ethereum.

- Tokens: Building applications on top of existing blockchains, often Ethereum-based examples, like UNI, LINK, and DAI.

Volatility

- Coins and utility tokens: they usually attract quite great vulnerability to volatility, mainly due to the nature of supply and demand on the market.

- stablecoin can only serve to preserve the value, which is sometimes pegged onto the value of a fiat currency, such as that old good USD.

- Privacy Coins: They tend to attract regulatory action, hence volatile also.

Regulative Environment:

- Payment Coins: It is accepted by some governments and companies, though, nearly all face regulatory questions from everywhere.

-Stablecoins: Conversely, increasingly regulated, with more pegging against fiat currencies in value and for use in decentralized finance.

- Privacy Coins: These are often subject to far greater regulation, if not outright bans, in many cases, due to features of anonymity that may make them a target for AML laws.

Conclusion: In fact, there are several different kinds of cryptocurrencies, and the underlying technology for one differs from that for another. Each of these is for a different purpose and therefore utilizes different underlying technologies. Coins would include Bitcoin or Ethereum, blockchains unto themselves either for value storage or as means of a transaction. Tokens exist on top of an existing blockchain and are meant to provide special functions for governance, utility, or even joining DeFi. Under this, it will help you determine the exact type that suits your needs - whether an investment, transactional, or to take part in various purposes in decentralized platforms.

36..What are the different uses of Cryptos?

The use of Cryptocurrencies can be wide in functionality and application. Some of the main uses include:

1. Digital Payments
Description: The main use of cryptocurrencies has been done to pay for goods and services on online websites and some particular physical stores.
Examples include: BTC - Bitcoin; LTC - Litecoin; BCH - Bitcoin Cash.

2. Store of Value
Description: Some of the digital currencies are a store of value; therefore, they are used like gold to hedge against either inflation or economic instability.
- Examples: Bitcoin (BTC), which is often referred to as "digital gold."

3. Investment and Trading
Description: The biggest investors invest in buying cryptocurrencies and holding in order to increase value over a period of time. Traders will buy or sell these based on expectations of profitable values.
Examples include but are not limited to: Bitcoin BTC and Ethereum ETH or ALTCOINS.

4. Smart Contracts
-Description: Blockchain cryptocurrency enables one to create and then execute smart contracts. Smart contracts are the contracts that automatically can implement themselves with pre-agreed terms written directly into lines of code.
- Examples: Ethereum allows for decentralization of applications, or even deploying smart contracts on the network.

5. Decentralized Finance (DeFi)
Description: Let me explain in simple terms what cryptocurrency is for inclusive decentralized finance. It performs a supporting role, usually by conventional intermediaries, in facilitating activities relating to lending, borrowing, and trading.
Examples include AAVE from Aave and Compound's COMP. They let unleased, decentralized functioning of lending and borrowing fall into place.

6. Tokenization
Tokens in cryptocurrency might replace some forms of other assets or some forms of ownership, for example-including but not limited to real estate, art, and other material possessions.
Other examples include the tokenization of assets on Ethereum or Polkadot blockchain.

7. Governance and Voting
- Description: Some cryptocurrencies give their holders voting rights or even participated in some project or protocol governance in a decentralized manner.
Examples of such include the MKR token that grants holders voting rights over changes proposed to be made on MakerDAO.

8. Confidentiality and Anonymity
Description: Some designs of cryptocurrency are invested in the significant elaboration of methods to raise the level of privacy and anonymity while doing a transaction, what in turn makes tracking

information about the transaction impossible.
Examples are Monero (XMR), and Zcash (ZEC).

9. Cross-border transactions

Description: Some crypto can enable international money transfer with no involvement of banks, hence no banking fees. In addition, it is way faster.
Examples include Ripple XRP and Stellar XLM.

10. Charitable Contributions

Description: Cryptocurrencies have found their place in philanthropy; it allows donors to make fast and transparent transactions.
Examples are legion: most charities today take Bitcoin and other cryptocurrencies.

11. Online Gaming and Virtual Goods

Description: The usage of the cryptocurrency has been extended towards gaming platforms for purchasing virtual goods, items inside games, and even as a way of rewarding players using virtual goods.
Examples include Enjin Coin, which is applied in gaming on blockchains.

12. Identity and Authentication

Description: Needless to say, digital identity management and user authentication across a number of systems would follow quite easily with the facilitation provided by cryptocurrencies and blockchain.
- Examples: Solutions like Sovrin and SelfKey have been building solutions on decentralized identity.

13. Supply Chain Management

Description: Blockchain cryptocurrencies allow tracing every supply chain process and its management in order to ensure that goods have minimum guarantees related to transparency and authenticity.
Examples are VeChain, applied in extending the supply chain by improving its capability for origin view and traceability.

14. Crowdfunding and Fundraising

Description: Initial Coin Offerings, commonly abbreviated as ICO, are a means of raising capital in cryptocurrency form, desired for new projects and startups.
Some of those examples include Chainlink LINK and Filecoin FIL, which have already been issued by their respective ICOs.

Events of these kinds basically act as a testament to the capability and influence of cryptocurrencies in the monetary, technical world, and even digitization of supply chain and identity.

37..Difference between cryptos coins versus tokens.

While the terms crypto coin and crypto token are used interchangeably, there are ostensible differences between them on the basis of their functions and applied technology.

1. Crypto Coin:

Native to Its Blockchain: A crypto coin is an innate digital currency of a particular blockchain.

Examples are that Bitcoin (BTC) is a native coin of the Bitcoin blockchain, while Ether (ETH) serves as a native coin for the Ethereum blockchain.

- Purpose: The general purpose of any coin is normally to pay for something, a store of value, or an account unit. They might be used for paying transaction fees, mining rewards to participants in the network, and to store value like money.

Examples include Bitcoin, normally abbreviated as BTC, Ether normally abbreviated as ETH, Litecoin normally abbreviated as LTC, and Binance Coin normally abbreviated as BNB.

2. Crypto Token:

Existing Blockchains: "Basically, a crypto token is an issue of some kind of digital asset on top of an already existing blockchain-usually based on smart contracts ". Most of the tokens are built on the Ethereum blockchain with the ERC-20 standard.

-Purpose: The purpose of a token might be many-sided, too: to give representation for assets like land or some kind of equity, some kind of means of getting access to services or platforms, and even some kind of governance token in some DApps. Most of them are used in some ecosystems or for some uses. Examples include, but are not limited to, the following: USDT, LINK, UNI, and all ERC-20 or BEP-20.

Difference between:

Blockchain Dependency: Coins belong to their blockchain, but tokens depend on the blockchain of some other cryptocurrency.

Purpose: The most direct use of coins is that they are used as a form of money or currency, while tokens are representatives of various kinds of wealth and rights.

In other words, though both are cryptocurrencies, the difference between tokens and coins is that while the latter denotes the basic cryptocurrency of the blockchain, the former functions at the back of any other blockchain and can represent anything from an asset to utility.

38..Buy crypto coins or crypto tokens?

Whether to invest in crypto coins or crypto tokens depends on an investor's goals, risk appetite, and understanding of the market. The following differentiation shall help clear your mind:

1. Crypto Coins:

Stability and Adoption: Very few coins, including but not limited to Bitcoin and Ethereum, have been better known and here longer; therefore, the scores of their adoption are high. Most of them tend to be more stable, especially with more long-term investments.

Use Case: Most of the coins have some kind of explicit purpose-be it transactional, a store of value, or for paying for transactional fees. For example, Bitcoin has been framed as "digital gold," while Ether has become key to interacting with the Ethereum blockchain.

Market Position: Most of the coins are in high positions within the market. Some even rank at the top when it comes to market capitalization. For that matter, one couldn't assume it would ever disappear completely.

2. Crypto Tokens:
From diversified usage-from the fact that tokens are stakes in projects and/or utility tokens to real-world assets and security tokens-some of them, including tokens of DeFi or NFTs, are also used as a means of exposing themselves to specific areas of the crypto market.

High Return Possibility: Tokens that are related to very promising projects or new technologies can promise high returns if the project happens to be successful. These usually also have higher risks due to the volatility factor and the 'project failure' factor.

Utility and Governance: There are some tokens that might have utilities specifically associated with being an owner that uniquely engages an owner, access to governance, access to a set of capabilities of a platform. If one believes in the future success of a platform or an ecosystem, it would, therefore be beneficial to hold on to its token.

Key Considerations:
-Risk Tolerance: On the whole, coins are considered to be less risky than tokens, which are very volatile and linked with the success of a particular project or technology.
-Investment Horizon: If you're looking at long-term stability, it might sit more comfortably with coins. If you seek a high but riskier return, it may be at the end of tokens.
-Project Understanding: Behind every token, there is an absolute need to go right into the guts of the project before making the purchase; getting background knowledge of the team, the technology, use case, and the demanded market.

Conclusion:
- Invest in a Crypto Coin: If you believe in more established and lower-risk investments in the long-term feasibility of major blockchains, such as Bitcoin or Ethereum.
-One should consider investing in Crypto Tokens if they have a higher risk appetite with a possibility of higher returns, and if something in the crypto arena draws your interest in certain sectors or projects.

Anyhow, it goes without saying that the secret of safely investing in cryptocurrency markets always lies in the diversification of your portfolio-investing sums such that, if lost, it would still remain affordable.

39..What are stable coins?
Stablecoins are forms of cryptocurrencies that are designed to be stable in value relative to a fiat currency or any other means that may act in its place as an asset. The main objective of the stablecoin is an attempt to combine almost all the advantages of cryptocurrencies, such as fast and free access anywhere in the world, with the stability of traditional money.

Types of Stable Coins

1. Fiat-Collateralized Stablecoins
- Description: These are fiat currency-reserve-collateralized stablecoins held within a bank or with an approved custodian. In theory, the supply of this type of stablecoin is as large as the number of

underlying fiat currencies purchased into custodial hands.

Examples include

- Tether (USDT): it is a cryptocurrency pegged to the US dollar, meaning that the quantity supposedly held in reserve is equal to the number of issued tokens outstanding.
- USD Coin: This one is also pegged to the US dollar and is audited regularly to prove its fiat reserve.

2. Crypto-Collateralized Stablecoins

Description: These are types of stablecoins that get their collateral backing from other cryptocurrencies, not of some forms of fiat currencies. Many of these are over-collateralized for their backing assets due to the volatility within them.

Examples include

- DAI: It is a cryptocurrency created on the MakerDAO system. It's a cryptocurrency collateralized by a basket of different cryptocurrencies regulated on the blockchain through smart contracts.
- sUSD: This is an over-collateralized stablecoin of many forms of cryptocurrency that have been wrapped into the Synthetix network.

3. Algorithmic Stablecoin

Description: Algorithmic stablecoins are those that are neither collateralized nor use any form of collateral. Instead, they rely on algorithms and smart contracts to control supply and always maintain their value at a constant level. They always automatically change the supply of a particular stablecoin when market demand needs them to do so.

- Examples:

-Ampleforth (AMPL): This is a digital asset that draws its stability from its elastic supply model.

-Terra, otherwise known as LUNA, is a method for combining a lot of algorithms and the native token LUNA to make the value of this cryptocurrency stable.

Applications of Stablecoins

1. Trading and Hedging

- Description: A trader uses a stablecoin to hedge against the volatility of the cryptocurrency market and for fast fund transfers across a number of exchanges or trading pairs.

Examples include but are not limited to avoiding direct exposure to the BTC or ETH volatility by using the USDT or USDC as base currency.

2. Payments and Transactions

- Description: Provides the ability to pay for and transact in values which are pretty stable, not as volatile as the cryptocurrency. They are useful in both personal and business applications.

Examples of these would be an online purchase in USDC and a cross-border transfer made through USDC.

3. DeFi - Decentralized Finance

- Description: DeFi platforms enable the lending and borrowing of stablecoin to generate interest, while ensuring stable value that unlocks the full range of financial services on a decentralized level.
- Examples include the use of the DAI, for example, within Aave or Compound lending protocols.

4. Saving and Investment

-Description: Stablecoins let one store value in a somewhat stable manner and, therefore, can be used for saving or investment, especially in decentralized savings accounts, or even in yield farming. Examples would include things like lending in stablecoin interest via DeFi protocols or savings accounts in some sort of stablecoin.

5. Cross-border transactions
-Description: Different use cases of stablecoins are available, including cross-border payment with negligible fees and speedier processing compared to traditional bank networks.
Examples include the use of USDT in international transfers or remittances.

6. Microtransactions in Gaming
-Overview: Stablecoin can be used for micron-transactions within online gaming or digital content where the money is stable enough for virtual purchasing or reward buying within that game.
Examples involve stablecoins being used for in-game purchases or rewards on a blockchain gaming platform.

Advantages of Stablecoin

- Stability: It can guarantee stability, unlike some very volatile cryptocurrencies.
-Liquidity: This refers to when it would be pretty easy to move from a conventional cryptocurrency into another one and back.
- Efficiency: Allow for creating low-cost, high-speed transaction capability, particularly in DeFi implementations.
- Transparency: Most of them have instituted transparent and frequent auditing processes, especially with the variants of fiat collateralized stablecoins.

It meets at a point with the conventional financial system and cryptocurrency by providing a means assured of its tool in various activities in finance.

40..Can I mix between the different coins?
You can mix conceptually between a variety of different cryptocurrencies in a number of ways, depending on what you are trying to achieve. Let's look at some common ones:

1. Sale and Purchase
Description: Most of these are obtained through trading or exchanging other kinds of cryptocurrencies in numerous exchanges. One can, for instance, sell Bitcoin and buy Ethereum or any other altcoin.
This is done most usability-wise through an exchange website, such as Coinbase, Binance, or Kraken, where one exchanges any given cryptocurrency into another.

2. Portfolio Diversification
Description: diversification of your portfolio is a balance to strengthen your risk management and investment opportunities in the cryptocurrency market. That simply means you'll be able to invest in all types of coins, balancing possible returns with potential risks.
How to Diversify Your Portfolio: To hold more than at least one cryptocurrency; for example, Bitcoin and Ethereum, plus all the altcoins.

3. DeFi Platforms
Description: Most of the DeFi applications will enable your wallets to be used in multiple

cryptocurrencies for one kind of financial activity: lending, borrowing, or yield farming. Utilize DeFi protocols such as Uniswap or Aave; these support a wide range of different cryptocurrencies for trading or earning interest.

4. Cross-chain transactions
Description: It is a way that cross-chain transactions would be enabled, allowing users to interact with more than one blockchain or cryptocurrency. It could serve as a kind of bridge between assets on the various blockchains.
How to: Using cross-chain bridges, or any other services which may provide support for other cryptocurrencies, too, such as Binance Smart Chain Bridge.

5. Stablecoin Swaps
Flexibility: The ability to utilize or switch to other classes of stablecoin or some other form of cryptocurrency.
How to: The same may be done on certain popular platforms or exchanges that allow one to convert from one stablecoin into another. Say, one may change USDC for USDT.

6. Multiple currency wallets
Description: Some wallets are created in such a way that they are able to host more than one cryptocurrency. This helps in the ability to hold more than one coin or manage different types of coins within the same wallet.
How to store or manage different kinds of cryptocurrencies: to be kept within multi-wallets, such as Exodus or Trust Wallet.

7. Decentralized Exchanges (DEXs)
Description: DEXs are a mean for different classes of cryptocurrency to trade directly without the interference of any middlemen and normally support hundreds of tokens.
How to trade between tokens of different kinds using this very decentralized network? with the aid of DEX solutions like Uniswap or SushiSwap.

Things to Consider

- Fee: Note that the fee for transactions will differ between various exchanges and/or platforms.
- Safety: Let all the utilized platforms and wallets be well-recognized to avoid probable fraud or hacking cases.
- Liquidity has to be considered, whether the mixed-up cryptocurrencies have good liquidity or not. Some of them have a low trading volume or high slippage.

Mixing among cryptocurrencies, is a strategic approach toward handling one's portfolio of assets, in addition to diversification through varied investment opportunities to participate in different financial perspectives over the crypto space.

41..What are NFTs (Non fungible tokens) ?
NFT tokens are a form of digital assets that are a kind of title of ownership over some unique item or any other form of content, stored on some blockchain. The point is that, in contrast to all other cryptocurrencies-like Bitcoin and Ethereum-which could have been exchanged on an equal basis and were considered to be fungible, NFTs are non-fungible, and each token is different from the rest.

Some important features of NFTs are

1. Original:
While each NFT can be different from any other token because of metadata and attributes, it is this uniqueness that makes NFTs utilized for the representation of unique digital or physical items.

2. Indivisibility:
They are also indivisible: there is either the whole of it or nothing for any user. In fact, this is really opposite to cryptocurrencies, whereby one could divide into smaller fractions.

3. Ownership and Provenance:
NFTs are recorded on blockchains in standardized formats like ERC-721 or ERC-1155. The fact that they are recorded on blockchains makes ownership verifiable and provident-meaning their ownership history can be traced.

4. Interoperability:
Other platforms and marketplaces can be used alone or in totality. For example, an NFT minted on Ethereum can be bought, sold, or shown on any platform that supports Ethereum-based NFTs.

Use Cases of NFTs:

1. Digital Art:
Digital artwork is created in just one form in which only an artist can create a variant in the form of an NFT. They can be bought, sold, and owned; thus, it allows digital artists to monetize their work.

2. Antiques/Collectibles:
NFTs can be implemented in design and foundation for capturing other forms of digital collectibles, including, among others, trading cards or virtual pets. Examples include "CryptoPunks" and "CryptoKitties.".

3. Gaming:
The implication, in simple terms, is that tokenization of in-game assets for things like character skins or virtual land may be a form of NFT, which can then be freely owned and traded among players.

4. Music and Entertainment
Musicians and celebrities could also sell albums or concert tickets as NFTs-a new source of revenue that concurrently opens up new unique experiences for fans.

5. Virtual Real Estate:
Examples may be "Decentraland" and "The Sandbox", both of them are virtual worlds which make use of NFTs as proof of ownership for virtual land and property in their respective virtual worlds.

6. Identity and Membership:
Membership access, or even ID verification, might be opened for use by NFTs. Within them, the concreteness of rights regarding the enjoyment of certain services or communities would lie with the

owner of that particular NFT.

Overview:
NFT tokens are unique digital representations, majorly denoting ownership of something, whether items or content, on the blockchain. Many sectors so far have carried out their usage in artworks, collectibles, and gaming, among others. This is amongst the new ways of proving ownership and showing origin for both digital and physical assets.

42..What are DApps?

The short form DApps stands for "Decentralized Application"; thus, an application running on a decentralized network - like a blockchain - and not on a set of servers, in contrast to a centralized application. Those DApps work on P2P networks and depend on smart contracts to work without any intermediate and central authorities.

Here are the main features and characteristics of DApps:.

1. Decentralization is the most important reason DApps differ from other applications, as they work in a decentralized manner. They cannot work with central servers held by an entity, but on a blockchain or another type of DLT. In other words, there is no single owner controlling the system.

2. Open source:
Most of them are open-sourced, meaning any community can look over, change, or even improve the code. It is actually open-sourced in nature, hence tugging at trust because one can look over the smart contracts governing a DApp.

3. Smart Contracts
Applications make use of "smart contracts," which are self-executing contracts whereby the terms of an agreement are directly written into lines of code. They execute autonomously when certain conditions are met, and the rules therefore are enforced without an intermediary.
It can be some smart contract that is used to create some sort of logic, like lending or borrowing, for some DeFi-based DApp. No intervention of any bank shall be involved.

4. Blockchain-based
Usually, DApps run on top of public blockchains such as "Ethereum," "Binance Smart Chain," or "Solana." Of course, the most popular platform for DApps is Ethereum, due in large part to its original use case as a vehicle to implement smart contracts with its EVM, or Ethereum Virtual Machine.

5. Incentivization system tokens:
Most of the DApps have an internal economy or incentives system based on tokens, which is a form of cryptocurrency. Applications for tokens range from a value offering of the service by the DApp, in order to access the services offered by it, pay a transaction fee, reward and incentivize the users for their contributions to the network, and the developers themselves for their contribution in it.

6. Peer-to-peer interaction:
DApps allow for peer-to-peer interaction. For instance, in the case of a decentralized marketplace

dApp, trading and selling occur directly between individuals rather than through third-party marketplaces like Amazon or eBay.

Types of DApps:

The applications of DApps are many across several fields:

1. DeFi - Decentralized Finance
A few examples include Uniswap, Aave, and Compound.
DeFi DApps allow users to lend, borrow, trade, and invest in various cryptocurrencies without the interference of a financial middleman, such as banks or brokerages.

2. Gaming.
Examples include Axie Infinity and Decentraland.
In DApps-based blockchain gaming, this could be done by giving real ownership of the in-game assets to the participant himself, where these can be traded or sold out of the game environment.

3. Marketing Places: Examples of such include OpenSea and Rarible. These applications, on one side, will allow users to purchase and sell in decentralized ways, different types of digital assets, including "NFTs" or nonfungible tokens.

4. Social Networks: Examples include Steemit and Minds. Such platforms allow one to share content with a converse that is distributed, having no center authority controlling the flow of information.

5. Governance: Example: Aragon, Maker DAO. -Governance DApps: This just simply means a network of decentralized decision-making for companies; the token holder votes on proposals or changes to the platform.

Advantages of DApps include:

- Resistant to Censorship: Since they operate on top of decentralized networks, DApps are far less prone to censorship and never go down like centralized applications. The users also have more control over their data and properties since intermediary steps are usually removed. Due to the nature of the invention itself, creation in a manner that is open-source and peer-to-peer assures transparency, but so does the fact that they are DApps containing smart contracts.

Issues with the DApps:

- Scalability: Today, the scalability of DApps is quite poor since block chaining on networks hinders it. Congestion in the latter may finally end up with the consequence of longer transaction time and higher transaction fees relative to others. All in all, DApps are going to be way more complex to learn and probably won't stack up quite the same in terms of smooth experience compared with their traditional counterparts.

- Security Vulnerabilities: Though DApps are designed on a decentralized platform, the probability of having bugs in their smart contracts isn't ruled out. It usually gets attacked if such bugs are exploited, leading to stolen funds.

Conclusion: DApps are, in fact, decentralized systems, to give users more control, decentralization, and transparency. The common applications shared among them are financial uses, gaming, and digital marketplaces. They are set for the future in smart contracts operating on blockchain networks, such as Ethereum. There are associated scalability and user experience challenges, too.

43..Will Crypto go to zero?

The chances that all cryptocurrencies will go to zero are very low, even if a few, as individuals, might fail. Here's why crypto as a whole won't go to zero and what to consider:

1. Market Leaders: In this crypto space, there is only Bitcoin (BTC) and Ethereum (ETH) that ever led with huge market adoptions and technological developments. Institutional interest was good. Coupled with that, Bitcoin could be regarded as a means of storing value, while essentially being queued up as a comparison to digital gold, in finding out its implementation within companies such as Tesla, and further extended to countries like El Salvador. Ethereum has brought in a number of decentralized applications that include dApps, NFTs, and smart contracts, thereby enabling DeFi, so it forms the mainstay of the DeFi ecosystem. Large communities, huge infrastructures, and thereby huge adoptions-these are so big that the chances of these projects going to zero are minuscule.

2. Institutional and Corporate Interest. For example, the big banks are those adopting cryptocurrencies, incorporating it into their services, such as "PayPal, Visa, Mastercard,"Blackroch" and "JPMorgan.".
While governments and central banks are nowadays studying and embracing blockchain technology within the so-called Central Bank Digital Currencies, other companies like "Square (now Block)" and "MicroStrategy" have been aggressive with investments in Bitcoin. Institutional interest stabilizes the market and ensures that it does not experience a complete collapse.

3. Other application examples, other than a speculative use. In fact, cryptocurrencies can be used for more than just trading speculation. Here are some examples of their uses:

-DeFi enables lending, borrowing, and trading by users directly, without the interference of any other agent.

-NFT's: It is about the ownership of digital pieces, such as pieces of art, gaming-related elements, and even collectibles.

-Cross-border: Bitcoin and other cryptos, including Ripple XRP and Stellar XLM, are struggling to find ways of making international transfers cheaper and faster.

-Supply Chain and Data Security: Blockchain improves the supply chains by creating a generation of transparency, and it is also good for data protection. Applications such as these show that the utility of crypto can extend past investments, hence their potential to be completely obsolete is zero.

4. Regulation by the States: Where regulation may increase, it is far from a likelihood that all crypto shall be banned or go to zero. Most countries are still finding ways of regulating the use of crypto and not banning its use altogether. Regulation may also lead to higher adoption and thus stability. Whereas a few countries, like China, have banned crypto, countries like the United States, Europe, and Japan are working out the basic mechanism for crypto usage which would be beneficial to the investors.

5. Volatility vs. Market Collapse: Cryptocurrency markets are really volatile. Sometimes, the swing in prices becomes so wild that the value of individual cryptos hugely decreases, or just becomes worthless, sometimes even called a "rug pull," or, by projects that have failed to develop well. But going to zero is different than volatility. Settled cryptos, such as Bitcoin and Ethereum, have been pretty rugged against any large downturns and have always recovered in history.

6. Potential of Risk: It is not likely that all the available cryptocurrencies will zero out, but some risks and complications to the market are categorized and outlined as follows:

-Overload Regulation: The numerous strict regulations all over the world concerning the usage of privacy coins/stablecoins may lead to decreased liquidity and participation.

-Eventual Technological Failure or Security Breach: Sometimes huge bugs or hacks may happen in the underlying blockchain, which can result in a loss of confidence.

-In the case of a great global financial collapse, or in case of loss of confidence in digital assets, this could be really bad for the industry.

- Market Saturation: The recent projects and new tokens go on to be overhyped, which at times causes some of the projects and new tokens to collapse. However, this is in relation to those cryptocurrencies that are of a lesser nature and less established.

Conclusion: Some will break and disappear, but all of them going to zero is impossible. The robustness in crypto has been through many reasons, like big and well-performing projects, real-case applications, and increasing institutional and technological adoptions, which enabled it to sustain itself. But one crypto may break, so the investor should try to do comprehensive research on the project and diversify.

44..Can I spend crypto like cash?
No, cryptocurrencies are not "fiat money". The difference is as follows:

Fiat Money: A form or type of money whose value is derived from the fact that the government declares it to be so while believing in its legitimacy. Examples include the US dollar, the euro, or the Japanese yen. Fiat money is a form of legal tender and is legally recognized by the government in the discharge and settlement of debts for goods and services.

Cryptocurrency: This is a kind of decentralized, digital currency neither any, nor all governments of the world have issued or supported. Values depend on supply and demand in the market and are not considered legal tender in most places, aside from Bitcoin in El Salvador.

While it can be used in some point-of-sale situations, it doesn't hold the same status in most countries neither by legality nor stability. As a matter of fact, this already makes them another class of currency and not convertible in most contexts with money per se.

45..Can I get a crypto debit or credit card?
Yes, you can get a credit card or debit card linked with your cryptocurrency wallet. With the cards, one can spend his or her cryptocurrency everywhere any other credit or debit card is accepted, making the usage of crypto in everyday applications quite easy. Here's how they work and some of the popular options available:

1. Crypto Debit Cards
- How they work.
Crypto debit cards are basically a link to your cryptocurrency wallet: For each purchase, the card service would convert the required sum of crypto to fiat money, such as the USD or EUR, to pay for the merchant.
- Some of them allow you to independently convert your crypto to fiat in advance, while others automatically convert at the actual time of the transaction.

Most of them are pegged to major payment networks such as Visa or Mastercard, and thus they are almost universally accepted.

- Most popular crypto debit cards:
Coinbase Card: Well, this is the Visa debit card availed by Coinbase, and it works alongside spending cryptos directly from one's account. You choose what to spend in crypto, and it covers a wide range of cryptos, including Bitcoin, Ethereum, and many others.
Binance Card: This is currently available only in some regions. The Binance Visa Card is a way to spend your crypto directly from your Binance wallet, with cashback from purchases, while supporting a wide variety of cryptocurrencies.
Crypto.com Visa Card: Crypto.com has several Visa cards; each of them offers their holders some sets of benefits, such as cashback or subscription refunds, with access to airport lounges. This card will be directly attached to your Crypto.com Wallet, to which you can refill the balance in crypto.
BitPay Card: BitPay Mastercard is available in the United States. You can load up the balance in Bitcoins inside a card and a few other cryptocurrencies, which later can be utilized as the USD.

2. Crypto Credit Cards:
- How They Work:
Crypto credit cards work exactly like any other credit card but offer rewards in forms of cryptocurrencies and do not provide cashback or points.
Most of these cards would require fiat currency in order to pay off the credit balance owed, while several will indeed allow someone to make use of crypto in order to pay off the outstanding balance.

- Major Crypto Credit Cards:
* BlockFi Rewards Visa® Signature Card: This card pays in the form of Bitcoin rewards. You earn a percentage of your spending back in Bitcoin, which goes directly into your BlockFi account. There are no annual fees, and rewards can be higher for specific categories.
• Gemini Credit Card: A credit card that Gemini issues to pay you back, in Bitcoin or some other cryptocurrencies, for as much as 3% of your purchases into your Gemini account.
* SoFi Credit Card: This card by SoFi has cashback rewards that, if you have a SoFi account, are convertible into cryptocurrency, without annual fee.

3. How to Get a Crypto Card:
- Usually, it's directly on platforms which issues such kind of a card: Coinbase, Crypto.com, and Binance.
Some of the most common conditions to use them are hereby mentioned:

-KYC Verification: Most of the platforms require you to go through some sort of Know Your Customer verification process, where you have to give out a number of personal information and supporting documents about yourself to validate your identity.
- Link Your Wallet: In some of these cards, you have to link your crypto wallet or fund the card with cryptocurrency directly from your account.
- Card issuance: Once approved, the physical card will be dispatched from the platform, although a few of them offer a virtual card that can be utilized on the spot.
- Spending: It also integrates all the major mobile applications to track your expenditure, claims rewards, and converts crypto into fiat.

4. Crypto Cards: Their Key Benefits
- Ease of Use: Those cards will make spending with crypto as effortless as spending with cash, not taking any advance care of converting your crypto into fiat money.
- Rewards: Most crypto cards offer different types of rewards by using your card, allowing you to earn more crypto with greater usage.
- Global Acceptance: Considering it mostly comes with the association of either Visa or Mastercard, this is also commonly accepted in most merchants around the globe.

5. Considerations:
- Various fees could be included in the conversion, use of an ATM, and issuance of your card.
- Tax Implications: In several jurisdictions, spending crypto is considered a taxable event because it implies the sale of crypto assets. Keep track of transactions for tax reporting, if needed.
- Availability: In some regions or countries, not many crypto cards are available. That alone means, depending on your location, it may not be available for you.

Conclusion:
Yes, you can have a credit or debit card that allows you to spend cryptocurrency directly from your wallet. An ever-growing number of such cards helps you to easily include crypto in your daily life. Yet more to that: there are things to consider, such as fees, taxation, and places where the card will be usable.

46..Can I use cryptocurrencies worldwide?
Although cryptocurrencies can be used anywhere in the world, its use and legality vary from country to country. Some of the critical considerations are as follows:

1. Cross-border transactions:
For one thing, cryptocurrencies such as Bitcoin and Ethereum can be freely transacted across borders, sent, and received without the need, interference, or involvement of banks and traditional financial intermediaries. This is the very reason why they have, hitherto, emerged to serve as workable alternatives for international transactions and remittances.

2. Legal and Regulatory Differences:
Crypto-friendly countries are those that have taken up the use of cryptocurrencies and allowed them to be in wide usage. Countries like the United States, Canada, Japan, and even Germany allow these in various forms of transactions from time to time with regulation.
Constrained Countries: Some other countries have either implemented strict restrictions on crypto usage or a full ban on it. For instance, China has completely banned trading and mining of any form of cryptocurrency, while in India, the stands over the issue of regulation have been fluctuating.
Taxation and Reporting: A lot of countries have legalized the usage of crypto, though one might have to report for taxes since it is viewed as an asset, much like stocks.

3. Merchant Acceptance:
But theoretically, as much as cryptocurrency could be applied all over the world, it is still, up to a certain degree, dependent on whether merchants would accept it or not. It is accepted in some big companies and online platforms, but it may be unacceptable to the small ones or locally-owned businesses.

4. Volatility:
Sharp volatility within the big up-and-down swings in the price of cryptocurrencies, could make them unsuitable for everyday purchases, even in countries with a relatively stable local currency.

5. Matters relating to cross-frontier issues
While cryptocurrencies operate across borders, one does find some annoyance converting it into local fiat currencies, mainly in countries which have banned or even over-regulated exchanges.

In other words, though cryptocurrencies may be global, their actual application once again is at the mercy of local legislation, the degree to which they are adopted by merchants, and the degree to which they can be immediately and effortlessly turned into fiat money in a country.

47..Can I borrow money using cryptos?
Yes, you can borrow some fiat money against the placement of your cryptocurrency as collateral through several platforms and services. In fact, some even refer to this process as "crypto-backed loans" or "crypto-collateralized loans." Here is how it works and everything you should know:

1. How Crypto-Backed Loans Work:
- Collateral: You deposit some sum of cryptocurrency into the lending platform, say Bitcoin or Ethereum, against which, in turn, works as collateral to the loan.
- Loan-to-Value Ratio: The amount of fiat a person can borrow is usually a portion of the collateral's value. It is referred to as the Loan-to-Value, or LTV ratio. If the LTV is 50%, and for example, a person deposits $10,000 worth of Bitcoin, then he or she will be credited with a maximum of $5,000 in fiat.

- Interest Rates: The interest is to be paid on the fiat lent. It might differ for different platforms depending on the LTV ratio and the type of cryptocurrency taken against the loan.

-Repayment: It simply means returning the loan amount with the interest included in it within the stipulated time period. Once you return the loan, then the collateral will be returned to you.

-Margin Calls: That is when the value of your collateral has contracted, the LTV ratio has shrunk, and now the platform is going to grant a margin call for you to add more collaterals or pay off partial debt in order for the required LTV ratio to be maintained. It's at this stage that the platform instantly liquidates your collateral against returning the loan amount if its request is not met.

2. Where to Get a Crypto-Backed Loan:
- Centralized Lending Platforms:

- BlockFi: The lender offers USD loans with Bitcoin, Ethereum, or any of the supported cryptocurrencies availed as collateral. Terms vary on interest rates and LTVs.
- Nexo: Offers instant crypto-collateralized loans in more than 40 different fiat currencies. Nexo allows for flexible repayments, plus competitive interest rates.
- Celsius Network: the user gets to borrow fiat or stablecoins against their crypto assets with variable LTVs and interest rates.
- Decentralized Finance (DeFi) platforms:
Aave is a DeFi lending market; this is a place where one lends money in stablecoin or any other form against his running cryptocurrency on Ethereum Blockchain with smart contracts.
- Compound: Another widely used DeFi protocol that enables users to borrow against their crypto collateral in fiat-pegged stablecoins, such as USDC or DAI.
- MakerDAO enables Ethereum deposits to be made in order to mint DAI, a stablecoin whose value is pegged to USD. Not technically fiat, but easily convertible to fiat on many of the leading cryptocurrency exchanges.

3. Benefits of Crypto-Backed Loans:
- No Credit Check: Most of the platforms would not require a credit check as long as there was collateral to cover the loan, hence opening it to more classes of borrowers.
- Fast Access to Liquidity: Draw on fiat liquidity without necessarily needing to sell off your cryptocurrency, should you happen to feel that your crypto is going to appreciate in value over time. Everything can be very flexible, starting with the interest rates, which may be variable or fixed, right to the time span for paying off the loan.

4. Some Risks to Keep in Mind:
- Volatility: The value of your cryptocurrency collateral might experience a violent change in the wrong direction, and could be subject to either a margin call or liquidation.
- The rate of interest for some of these platforms could be very high, considering the already high LTV ratio.
- Centralized platforms would also mean that one would have to trust the company with his collateral. Their failure or bankruptcy presents a risk, whereas DeFi platforms depend on smart contracts, which themselves can be vulnerable.

Conclusion
A crypto-backed loan is great in such cases, when one needs liquidity but does not want to sell his cryptocurrencies. But one needs to be crystal clear regarding the terms and risks involved besides the volatility in the crypto market before going ahead with the crypto-backed loan.

48..Can I earn interest with crypto? What is stacking?
Yes, you can definitely develop interest from a cryptocurrency portfolio. Here's a high-level overview of the most common methods of developing interest on your crypto holdings.

1. Crypto saving accounts:
-Centralized platforms allow for the depositing of your cryptocurrency into some sort of account, where over time, interest is earned on your deposit-much like a regular savings account.
- BlockFi-Interest Bearing Accounts: Not just in Bitcoin and Ethereum, but even in a number of stablecoins, too. The interest rate does depend on the asset type and size.
- Nexo: Interest is paid on a wide range of cryptocurrencies and stablecoins at better rates if one

chooses to receive it in NEXO tokens.
- Celsius Network: This platform allows users to receive interest in their deposited crypto and at the best rates, which could be paid out even on a weekly basis.

How It Works: Most will lend out the deposited cryptocurrency to institutional borrowers or find a way to generate yield with it. Interest, very often earned, is compound in nature and is paid out, at times week to week or month to month.

2. Decentralized Finance (DeFi) Lending:
Lending protocols are DeFi platforms where one gets direct and decentralized access to his crypto assets, lending them out to other users, where you get awarded the interest: e.g., Aave, Compound, and MakerDAO.
- Aave: The opportunity to deposit cryptocurrencies into the liquidity pools of this platform, to gain interest. Supported assets move with variable and stable interest rates, moving within a big variety.
- Compound: You earn interest, which is to be in the same token you deposited into the Compound protocol. The interest rates move by the demand and supply happening on their lending market.
- MakerDAO: You have your Ethereum locked into the generation of DAI at MakerDAO and lend out the DAI at other platforms for interest.

How it works: DeFi lending is based on smart contracts that regulate the whole processing concerning loans and their repayments with interest. There are no middlemen in this process. The interest rate can be higher than that compared with traditional platforms but is highly volatile at the same time.

3. Staking
Generally speaking, staking means active participation via some sort of Proof of Stake, or other consensus mechanism, that involves the locking in of some quantity of cryptocurrency in a virtual wallet, to contribute to a network, through transaction validation and blockchain security. The compensatory rewards or even interests for such action come afterward. It could be an option for a network that could be kept secure while being less power-consuming compared to the proof-of-work systems. There are some big differences among cryptocurrencies as far as staking requirements and reward structures go.

Proof-of-Stake Cryptocurrencies: Many different cryptocurrencies have been using the Proof-of-Stake consensus mechanism, wherein a user is allowed to "stake" their coins and participate in the validation of transactions running on that network. When you do this, you get paid for your participation in the network's reward system through that cryptocurrency.
- Ethereum 2.0: Staking on the Ethereum 2.0 network was made possible with a stake of the ETH and getting a certain percentage as the staking reward. Commonly, this involves a lock-up of the ETH, as common in many other Proof of Stake cryptocurrencies.
-Cardano-ADA: Cardano allows you to delegate your coins to any staking pool in the network, whereby you will gain all the rewards that pool has earned without requiring you to run a full node.
- Similarly, much like Cardano, on Polkadot, users have the ability to stake DOT and earn block rewards through involvement in the consensus process on the network.

- How it works: Staking is the process of locking your coins in a wallet, contributing to network security and operations. Many are incentivized by a portion of block rewards, often paid out at some intervals.

4. Yield Farming:

- Liquidity provision: within DeFi you are allowed to provide liquidity to any DEX, like Uniswap for instance, or SushiSwap, or even PancakeSwap, and in return, take a due share of transaction fees, which sometimes get topped up with token rewards.
- Uniswap: In return for lending your crypto pairs in the Uniswap liquidity pools, you earn back some compensation through the trading fees, proportional to your contribution in the pool.
- SushiSwap: It is very similar to Uniswap, except with added incentives by way of SUSHI tokens.
- PancakeSwap can supply coins to the pools available on Binance Smart Chain in order to get interest or rewards.

- How it works: Yield farming concerns depositing one's assets into liquidity pools; the given action allows for trading at DEX. It is an idea of high return; but, at the same time, the risks are enormous due to far-flung market volatility and other risks which may appear in an instance, such as impermanent loss.

5. Dividend Paying Tokens:
- Interest-paying token: Some of the platforms give out tokens, which are representatives of the underlying assets deposited and accrue interest on their own.
- Compound cTokens - These are tokens that you get after depositing your assets into Compound. cDAI is an example. They are generally going to go up in value over time as interest accrues.
- Aave: Also, this gives you a token representing on-chain accruals of interest in real time.

How It Works: Through tokens that grow in value or quantity, because of the earned interest gained, those can, therefore, be kept in your wallet and earn interest.

6. CeFi vs DeFi: Considerations
CeFi: This means the funds and activities are processed by BlockFi, Celsius, and Nexo using their own resources. Generally speaking, this would mean better support, less risk of smart contract bugs, but there is counterparty risk, which means the possibility of a fall of the platform itself.
DeFi: All the services of DeFi go decentralized, and smart contracts lie at the very heart of making any decision regarding funds management. It returns higher control and very often yields, but it also increases risks due to smart contract vulnerabilities and market fluctuations.

Conclusion:
You may earn interest in a crypto portfolio in a number of ways: with the use of a centralized savings account, DeFi lending, staking, yield farming, or holding interest-paying tokens. Each of these bears a different risk-reward profile, and exhaustive research into their security, liquidity, and even the reputation of the platform will be in order before any large commitments of your assets are made.

49..Will governments adopt crypto?
It would only be that some aspects of cryptocurrencies would be adopted by governments; even fewer of them would actually go on to employ a full-scale, already well-settled, decentralized cryptocurrency

such as Bitcoin or Ethereum. Most governments have released or are on to their respective CBDCs (Central Bank Digital Currencies). Here's a snapshot of how things are shaping up:

1. Central Bank Digital Currencies:
Many governments at least theoretically weigh, if not actually play, with "CBDCs" (virtual versions of fiat currency issued and regulated by a nation's central bank). These would boast all sorts of advantages of the cryptocurrencies, like faster digital payments, but would yield not one iota of government control over monetary policy. Examples already include:
- China's Digital Yuan: Already at the pilot phases in China, with many looking at it as a full-on CBDC that is going to see wide dissemination over the course of the next couple of years.
- It is said that, at the moment, the European Central Bank conducts research related to finding ways to use digital currency for the Eurozone.
- US Federal Reserve: There is talk for the US to create a digital dollar; if there is to be one, they are at the very early beginnings of that decision.

2. Start of adoption of the Blockchain Technology:
This is while governments have increasingly shown interest in the use of blockchain technology to improve transparency and efficiency through better security in such systems as land registries, supply chains, and even voting systems. That does not necessarily translate into the adoption of cryptocurrencies in their current form.

3. Regulations around Cryptocurrencies:
From permission to use the cryptocurrency, provided that certain preconditions set forth by the relevant law are observed, up to the complete ban on the use of the latter in certain contexts-for example, as part of anti-money laundering or tax evasion. Already, many governments have promulgated, or are currently promulgating, regulatory regimes that permit consumers to make use of cryptocurrencies, although often with additional tax or reporting obligations being imposed.

4. Barriers to Adoption:
- Decentralized: Most cryptocurrencies work on decentralized networks devoid of a single governing body. Because of this, most governments will find it very hard to flex muscles in this sphere.
- Volatility: The wild swings in the prices of virtual currencies, including Bitcoin, make them unsuitable for general use as a national form of money.
- Monetary Policy: It will drastically reduce the authority of any monetary policy, including money supply and interest rates, that various governments utilize to keep their economies in check.

5. Countries Utilizing Crypto:
Very few countries have legalized Bitcoin as legal tender, such as "El Salvador", where people can use it together with and never in lieu of a country's legally recognized currency. That is very rare, and even in El Salvador, the process of adoption in places has been both painful and sometimes not successful.

Overview
- Centralized Adoption: This approach would mean taking into consideration that the government might go for CBDCs, or government-controlled digital currencies, as opposed to going toward totally decentralized cryptocurrencies.
- Controlled Usage: After that, this cryptocurrency use would be regulated by governments in order to curb the potential problems that may arise, including money laundering, tax evasion, and loss of control

over the economy.
- Blockchain Innovation: While possibly not something quite palatable to governments to engage fully in with decentralized cryptocurrencies, the concept does have some merit that can be utilized through the associated technology called blockchain for many purposes.

We won't see a complete movement of governments toward cryptocurrencies but a high interest in the usage of digital currencies to explore and innovate on blockchains.

50..Is it worldwide adopted?

Cryptocurrency is still growing in its acceptance across the international world; however, it has yet to reach international applications. Following are the general trends:

1. Geographical Variation: While many countries, such as El Salvador, which has even adopted Bitcoin as legal tender, and Nigeria, for example, where crypto adoption runs much deeper, sometimes as a consequence of inflation, economic instability, or a complete lack of access to traditional banking, other countries have strict regulations or outright bans, as in China.

2. Institutional Interest: Many institutional investors have been dipping deeper into levels of investment in crypto; corporations, and governments alike. Huge corporations like Tesla and PayPal have already begun to use cryptocurrencies, with a growing interest in CBDCs.

3. Public Awareness: While the awareness has reached a high, the actual usage is concentrated in niches such as investment, remittances, and DeFi. For most, crypto remains speculative rather than a means of paying.

4. Regulatory Environment: Governments and financial institutions of diversified parts of the world have given birth to a great deal of diversified regulatory frameworks. The regulatory uncertainty is one of the biggest barriers/ drivers of adoption.

That means that while crypto certainly is a growing force, it isn't at true mass adoption just yet.

51..Can it be duplicated?

No. Its very rare nature," the underlying blockchain technology" makes it impossible-in the classical word sense-to duplicate cryptocurrencies. Here's why:

1. Blockchain and Decentralization:

Cryptocurrencies do rely on blockchains that attain decentralization, having scattered records of practically all types of transactions across active networks of nodes. Explaining further, each transaction gets verified in the blockchain, and from then on, when the moment the block is completely full of transactions, it reaches the chain so that no other transaction gets tampered with or duplicated.

2. Double-Spending Problem:

Among the big problems being faced by digital currencies, there is a problem of so-called 'double spending'; or somebody who actually could use one and the same digital coin twice. Cryptocurrencies like Bitcoin avoid the problem of double-spending using a consensus mechanism, usually either Proof of Work or Proof of Stake, which ensures that multiple network participants attest to and add into the blockchain new transactions, excluding duplicates.

3. Cryptographic Security:

Cryptocurrencies depend upon strong cryptographic algorithms that protect the wallets and the transactions of coins or tokens. Most cryptocurrencies are unique pieces of data representing every coin or token in existence. Private keys are used in order to authorize transactions. Access to a private key is required in order to mint counterfeit coins, which is virtually impossible.

4. Immutable:

This also means that once a transaction is committed onto the blockchain, it cannot be reversed. This means that once a transaction has occurred, there is no way it can be reversed or changed. This is a prevention against the duplication or double-spending of cryptocurrency once the exact same type of cryptocurrency has already been in a valid transaction.

5. Possible risks:

While digital currencies as such cannot be copied, there are a few possible dangers in these aspects of:

Forking: Most of these cryptocurrencies allow for a certain form of forking in practice-a period of time when one has two blockchains. The usual consequence would be that of the replication of tokens on the two chains, with them subsequently being considered as two different tokens after the fork itself has occurred.

Hacks/Exploits: Thievery of cryptocurrencies either through hacking into exchanges or people's wallets has happened, but there is no actual duplication of coins; the hacker merely takes ownership of the coins.

Conclusion:

Because of the blockchain technology, cryptography, and consensus mechanism involved in digital currencies, they just can't be copied. In fact, considering the security protocols put up by the system, the chances of coin duplication within one blockchain are close to zero, with only a few edge cases such as forks.

52..Is cryptocurrency taxed?

Yes, most governments do impose a tax on cryptocurrency trading. Since the surrounding tax environment does change from time to time, and there is a huge difference in the approach between countries, a general view would be thus:

1. Types of Taxes Levied

- Capital Gains Tax: - Gains from the sale or exchange of any cryptocurrency shall be subjected to tax, depending on how much the gains in the value of an investment in cryptocurrency have appreciated over and above what was originally used to buy it.

Applicability: Most countries look at cryptocurrency gains as capital gains no different than stocks or real estate. That may also depend on the period of time for which the asset has been held: short-term versus long-term.

- Income Tax: Definition: Tax payable on such income received from cryptocurrency, be it in the form of wage or mining or staking reward.

Applicability: These are general areas in which ordinary income treatment has time and again come to fore, thus attracting taxation as such, in cases involving cryptocurrencies either as an issue in payment for services or as mining rewards.

- Transaction Tax: Definition: Most states impose some kind of tax on the transaction where a sale, purchase, or other forms of trade in cryptocurrencies are concerned.

Applicability: The same can be in the form of Value Added Tax, VAT, or Goods and Services Tax, GST, on all the transactions that concern cryptocurrency.

- Mining and Staking Tax: Taxation Definition: This is a form of taxation charged on all the benefits realized through mining or even staking of any digital assets. Proceed obtained are always under the capture of an income tax at its fair value.

Applicability: Depending on the jurisdictions, there will be a difference in the levy of tax on mining and staking rewards.

2. Examples:

- United States: Capital Gain: The IRS views cryptocurrency like any other asset. The gains made from sales, trade, or any other disposition of the assets apply as capital gains for tax purposes, utilizing one of the two long-term or short-term capital gain rates.

- Income: This may be income, which, on earning from employment, a person may receive in cryptocurrency or mining, is all ordinary income. It involves reporting by the taxpayers on their transactions and holdings in the cryptocurrency. Failure to do this means an imposition of penalties.

- The United Kingdom: Capital Gains: HMRC considers cryptos as a form of asset. On selling or exchanging cryptos, there is a tax on capital gains.

Income: Anything that one gets in the process of collecting or mining cryptocurrency is chargeable to income tax.

Reporting: Profits and gains relating to the cryptocurrency should be reported in the self-assessment tax return for the year.

- Canada Capital Gain: In the case of CRA, the cryptocurrency has been in relation to a commodity. Hence, any form of income that may be realized through sales or exchanging it, is a capital gain and liable under taxation.

Income: Revenue made through cryptocurrencies should be leveled with any other kind of income in view of tax incidence. The same happens with those that have been mined.

Reporting: this puts an obligation on the taxpayers' part to file all cryptocurrency transactions and incomes.

- Australia: Capital Gains: ATO considers digital currencies as property for taxation purposes. They would levy capital gains tax on any proceeds gained from the sale of crypto.

Income: It imposes an income tax on any form of income generated from cryptocurrencies, which in one way or another can be achieved by mining and staking.

Reporting: All about reporting cryptocurrency and other types of income.

3. Compliance and Reporting Recordkeeping: Records of cryptocurrency transactions are kept in high recordation; dates, amount, value at that particular time. These keep tracks and create the accuracy in the reports for tax purposes.

- Tax software: Many software packages are available that enable tracing, reporting, and valuation, among others, concerning cryptocurrency transactions for tax purposes. Professional Suggestion: Due to enormous taxes on cryptocurrency that almost change day in and day out, one should be updated about each single issue that pops up. It will always be worth it to consult some tax professional dealing in cryptocurrencies.

4. Regulatory Trends: Most of the countries are revising their regulations regarding cryptocurrencies with more lucidity. Even the regulatory bodies are getting focused on improving their levels of compliance and enforcement in the crypto space.

Future Amendments: Tax laws on cryptocurrencies will most probably be refined as markets mature, and more governments come up with comprehensive frameworks concerning digital assets.

Conclusion: Most of the world's governments are taxing every transaction in cryptocurrencies and deem them to be an income or capital gain depending on the situation. In this respect, clear perception and subsequent compliance with taxation policies on the part of any holder of cryptocurrencies, as defined by the law of his land, becomes important to keep him safe from potential penalties and to create accurate obligations.

53..Bitcoin or Fiat? (Government printed money)

A comparison between Bitcoin and fiat money, in this case, would deal more with an appraisal in terms of their respective roles, characteristics, and implications within the financial system. Bitcoin vs Fiat Money - Comparative Analysis:

1. Nature and Characteristics

Bitcoin:
- Bitcoin Digital Asset: Bitcoin is a kind of decentralized digital currency created on the backbone of blockchain technology. Bitcoin does not have a central governing body or main authority.

- Supply: It has a capped supply of 21 million coins, hence deflationary in nature. It mines new Bitcoins through mining till the cap is achieved.
- Transparency: Transactions in Bitcoin are recorded in a public ledger called blockchain. Since this ledger is pseudo-anonymous, the identity of participants or transacting parties isn't directly linked to the transactions.
- Volatility: Very volatile, the price of Bitcoin changes drastically in less than no time.

Fiat money:
- Traditional Currencies: Most fiat money draws their values from the economy of the issuing country. Traditional currencies include USD, or US Dollar, EUR or Euro, and JPY or Japanese Yen.
- Supply: As is evidenced by central banks, the fiat currencies can be printed and minted without limits and thus cause inflation once too much of the money is created.
- Centralization: All fiat money belongs to and is at the fiat of some central authority of any given government, through central banks, which pretty much regulate monetary policy, including interest and inflation.
- Stability: Most of these fiat currencies happen not to be as volatile as Bitcoin but rather exhibit behavior that is far from extreme. This is because they are influenced by a wide array of economic factors and government policies.

2. Uses and Acceptance

Bitcoin:
- Digital Deals: Using Bitcoin, one can go ahead and buy things online, invest in the same, store value just like the US dollar or any other globally recognized currency since most of the merchants and all the financial institutions enjoy wide acceptance.
- Investment: The usual term for Bitcoin would be speculative investment; it is even a source of digital storage of value, like "digital gold".
- Global Transactions: Bitcoin offers a way for individuals to conduct cross-border transactions directly with each other, cutting out all agents entirely, including banks.

Fiat Money:
- Daily activities: This is meant for everyday purchases of goods and services, to pay taxes, and to set aside for saving.
- Legal Tender: Since the government issues Fiat Currencies, therefore they are considered legal tenders that have to be accepted for the settlement of debts and also for paying taxes.
- Banking and Financial Systems: The entire previous banking system was based on the fiat currency, financial markets, and even government policies.

3. Safety and Risk

Bitcoin:
- Security: Ensure safe transactions of cryptocurrencies through the use of encryption algorithms together with the decentralized nature of blockchain. Possible security breaches could include hacking, loss of private keys, and even regulatory uncertainties.
- Risk: Bitcoin is subject to high volatility and speculative trading, which can lead to substantial financial risk.

Fiat Money:
- Security: Most of their security would emanate from the financial system and their treatment under the law of the country. They would be less vulnerable to most of the threats in the digital world, but they would remain highly vulnerable to physical theft and counterfeiting.
Additionally, depending on the tendencies of the governmental policy and global tendencies, such factors like inflation, devaluation, or instability of any fiat currency are possible.

4. Investment and Value Proposition

Bitcoin:
- Potential: Huge growth is expected from Bitcoin. It also serves for some investors as a hedge against inflation and economic instability. Value changes come through supply-demand forces and investor attitude.
- Adoption: This means the selling points of Bitcoin needed to make it valued decentralization, financial inclusion, and censorship resistance. It's still in the growth stage of the cycle just because while it is now being increasingly adopted, it remains a relatively new, evolving asset class.

Fiat money:
- Stability: By nature, Fiat money is stable and can easily be relied on for its value to be stored and used in transactions. They are supported in some way or another by the government's capability to lay and collect taxes and to steer monetary policy.
- Predictability: This would be predictable with the fiat currencies; they are regulated and hence, as it were, would turn out very stable at the base of the economy and the financial systems generally.

5. Legal and Regulatory Status

Bitcoin:
- Regulation: Bitcoin is decentralized, and there are many cases in which the regulation differs from one region to another, having a very complex ever-changing legal standing.
- Taxation: Bitcoin transactions may be liable for tax, depending on the country in which one operates, probably as capital gains or otherwise.

Fiat money:
- Regulation: All are well-regulated, as well as other fiat currencies, by a central bank, among other monetary authorities, in their issuance, flow, and even their floating exchange rate.
- Taxation: The use of the fiat currency is thus usually treated just about like any other fiat currency in that it would be subject to standard taxation and finances under the jurisdiction.

Conclusion:
Bitcoin is for cypherpunks, for investors in digital assets, for new fintech investors, and finally for those high-risk, high-reward guys, of which quite a healthy crowd exists. It also has enormous advantages from this domain, such as: decentralized, a possibly digital store of value among others. It is very volatile, and there is an enormous amount of regulatory uncertainty.
Fiat Money: Perfect for daily dealings, to put aside, or to invest in something stable. It's stable, having

legal recognition and embedding in traditional monetary systems, though facing issues like Inflations and Government controls.

But in the end, Bitcoin and fiat currency appeared to be two alternatives, and which of the two is to be used, depends on the person's financial objective and their risk tolerance when it comes to their strategy of investment. Most investors mix the two in search of a balancing act between stability and growth potential.

54..Safety of Bitcoin compared to fiat (Normal printed money):
The safety of cryptocurrency in opposition to cash depends on many factors.

1. Physical Theft: Cash has the tendency to get stolen physically or get misplaced. Cryptocurrencies are also not vulnerable enough in nature as far as physical theft is concerned, although the digital assets may get stolen for reasons relating to some sort of cyber-attack.

2. Digital Security: Digital security good habits play a very important role in the case of cryptocurrency in order to keep it out of reach of hacking, phishing, and malware, among others. Cash isn't burdened with these types of digital threats.

3. Protection under the Law: Most more traditional systems of banking have some forms of protection for both cash and bank accounts, such as deposit insurance. Since the cryptocurrencies are largely unregulated, most will not have similar protective measures in place.

4. Privacy: One who sought complete privacy would be able to maintain privacy to a degree with cryptocurrencies and simultaneously have all their moves traced on a blockchain. Cash transaction methods are private, though more easily lost or stolen.
Whereas the use of cryptocurrencies and cash come with their respective advantages and risks, proper management of either requires an understanding of, and mitigation against, its particular risks.

55..Bitcoin or Gold?
A comparison can be done with regard to nature, usage, and, most importantly, the role they play as types of investments. Here is a comparative view of the two:

1. Nature and Characteristics

Bitcoin:
- Digital: This is an example of electronic cash developed and controlled by blockchain technology.
- Supply: The supply of the cryptocurrency is capped at a maximum of 21 million coins; this, by default, makes Bitcoin a deflationary currency.
- Volatility: Bitcoin is highly volatile in terms of price; hence, a lot of ups and downs can be traced out within a very short period.
A feeling of ownership can also be achieved through the concept of the blockchain method of transaction system, brought into being by digital wallets.

Gold:
- Physical: Gold is a physical tangible commodity used through basic applications, including in

jewelry, consumer electronics, and investments.
 - Supply: Gold is almost a perfectly supplied good; it is a limited product, but there is mining of new refined gold, which is very time and cost consuming.
- Stability: It is perceived that gold is a much more stable store of value, than Bitcoin.
Ownership in this context can be understood to mean a state of possession, actual or through market instruments like gold ETFs and gold futures.

2. Use Cases

Bitcoin:
- Digital Transactions: The major use of Bitcoin is digital transactions, transferring value, and as a means of exchange.
- Store of Value: It has been considered some kind of a "store of value" or "digital gold"; thus, it is both scarce and decentralized.
- Investments: Many would be investing in it for the appreciation that it may bear with time, serving also as a hedge against traditional financial systems.

Gold:
- Uses: Behind gold speculation lies a purposeful, practical idea for the electronic industries, dentistry, and other similar industries that use this metal for its definite conductivity and malleability.
- Jewelry: This finds enormous applications in jewelry due to some aesthetical and physical properties.
- Store of Value: Conventionally, gold has been used as a hedge against inflation and economic instability. For ages, it has been considered a store of value and one class of a safe haven asset.

3. Nature of investment:

Bitcoin:
- Liquidity: Bitcoin can be easily traded on a variety of cryptocurrency exchanges 24/7.
- Accessibility: In that effect, investment in Bitcoin requires the need to buy a digital wallet and participation in cryptocurrency exchange.
- Regulation: It is also noticed that Bitcoin has fewer restrictions compared to the rest of the assets, so even though a bit riskier, its return might be high.
- Storage: It conclusively requires custodies in the digital space through wallets, hence are prone to cyberattack.

Gold:
- Liquidity: Gold is traded on major exchanges and thus the markets; physical gold can be sold or pawned.
- Liquidity and marketability: Diversification of the portfolio may be done either with real gold - bars or coins - or financial derivatives of it, like Gold ETFs and futures.
- Regulation: Gold markets are rather well regulated; therefore, protection for investors does exist.
- Storage: It is considered one of the main disadvantages of investment in gold; it needs to be kept in vaults, and one needs to bear some expenses in keeping it safe.

4. Historic Performance and Correlation

Bitcoin:
- Performance: Since its inception, Bitcoin has continued to provide radical surges in prices and therefore has grown considerably in the last years.
- Correlation: The return pattern of Bitcoin normally does not show a high correlation with the returns to other classes of assets, for instance, gold. This may thus act as a channel through which the investor can diversify his or her investments.

Gold finish:
- Performance: Traditionally, gold has been considered an investment that reaps its returns in the reasonably long term, and more often, appreciates in value during any level of economic crisis.
- Correlation: Traditionally, gold has a negative correlation with the return of traditional financial assets. In their analysis, the correlation of gold with Bitcoin falls in the range of low to moderate.

5. Risk and Considerations

Bitcoin Risk Factors:

 -Volatility: High price volatility leads to high losses or gains in the very short term.
- Regulation Risks: The regulative environment of Bitcoin is still at the initial development phase hence impacts its value and legal status.
- These are the two most common pitfalls of vulnerabilities that might make Bitcoin a target: hacking, and other software flaws in technology.

Gold:

- Deflation and Inflation: Normally, it is viewed that gold will not perform well during the cases of either deflation or high interest rates.
- Costs of Storage: Unlike digital gold, physical gold requires costs pertaining to its storage and insurance.
- Market risks: due to geopolitical confrontations and/or a change in the interest rate, among others.

Conclusion:
Whereas bitcoin is highly volatile with possible high returns, it is digital, decentralized, and invariably seen as a hedge and an investment for modern times. On the other hand, physical gold is something quite historical, having been in use for such a very long period as a hedge against inflation and other economic instabilities.
Depending on investor's investment goals, risk tolerance, and personal preference for either the modern-day digital asset or the traditional asset of gold, many investors always try to have a little of both, so that one may take advantage of the unique advantages that each possesses.

56..Invest in Bitcoin or Gold?
Whether buying Bitcoin or gold is better for the future has to do with your goals for investment, your acceptable level of risk, and your general observation of market trends. Here's a framework that can help:

1. Investment Objectives

Bitcoin:
- Growth Potential: If the requirement is for high growth potential, irrespective of the high volatility factor, then Bitcoin might be selected. To say the least, considering the surge over the last decade, high appreciation was witnessed in Bitcoin, and, at the same time considered highly risky, provided huge returns.
- Digital Assets Exposure: Bitcoin exposes an owner to the emerging class of digital assets and blockchain technology.

Gold:

Instead, if the stability and preservation of one's wealth would be at stake, in which case, gold is considered a haven, and a store of value, having an elaborate history. It is usually less volatile, serving as a hedge against inflation and recession.
- Diversification: Gold is one of the significant reasons for investment, as it actually enhances diversification in an investor's portfolio, especially in periods of poor economic performance or at times when other traditional assets perform inefficiently.

2. Appetite for Risk

Bitcoin:
High Volatility: Many times, the value of Bitcoin shoots up or touches the bottom within a very short span of time, hence, bringing enormous gains and colossal losses.
Regulatory and Technological Risks: The uncertainty in the regulation environment and potential technological vulnerabilities are concerns to Bitcoin.

Gold:
- Less Volatility: Normally, gold is less volatile than Bitcoin. The price changes smoothly and its graph is easier to predict.
- Market Risks: It is still going to be subject to general changes in interest rates, geopolitical events, and international changes in economic fortunes, though it is supposed to be one of the safer investments.

3. Trends continuing in the market and economic conditions

Bitcoin:
- Greater adoption, advancing technology, and most importantly, more clarity about regulations could drive the future of Bitcoin. In fact, as such assets get increasingly integrated into the financial system, Bitcoin might appreciate more.
- Volatility and speculation surround the Bitcoin markets, as nobody can tell what will happens with its future value amidst all the changes in regulations and market sentiments.

Gold:
- Inflation Hedge: Conventionally, gold is viewed as an inflationary hedge. If the rate of rise in the rate of inflation becomes manifold, then gold will provide shelter for value preservation.
Financial uncertainties-on the improbable occasion of something like an economic bust or financial crisis, gold is conventionally a good investment.

4. Investment Horizon

Bitcoin:
- Long-Term Potential: While huge potential for long-term growth exists with Bitcoin, this virtual currency is extremely volatile in the short run. If your investment strategy involves a longer investment horizon and can sustain jitters, Bitcoin could perhaps be apt.
- Emerging Asset: Bitcoin is relatively younger compared to gold, and its long-term function and stability are still in the process.

Gold:
- Long-term Volatility: Historically, gold has proved its worth for centuries and hence is considered long-term stable. Regarding this point, while talking about long-term stable investment and lower volatility, one should go for classic gold.

5. Diversification

Bitcoin:
- Diversification from Traditional Assets: Bitcoin can be added to one's portfolio in order to introduce diversification into a portfolio dominated by conventional assets of equity and fixed-income securities. This forms another asset class altogether, having its own characteristics.

Gold:
- Traditional diversification: over the years, gold has been part of most diversified portfolios available to the investor as protection against a wide variety of economic risks and market downturns.

Conclusion:

Invest in Bitcoin when one is after high growth with a stomach for high volatility and wanting exposure to digital assets and emerging technologies. Indeed, Bitcoin will find its perfect match only with those having a high tolerance for risk and correspondingly long-term investment horizons.

Invest in gold for stability, preservation of wealth, hedging of inflation, and economic uncertainty in the most conservative manners. It fits the investor who is after stability in his investment, not so volatile, and with a long history.

Most of the investors combine both in a way to balance growth potential with stability. Perhaps this may be a proper way of diversification which will offset some risks between the assets.

57..Crypto Adoption in the Future

The future adoption of cryptocurrency is foreseen as increasing, and some of the factors attributing to this fact include:

1. Increased Institutional Investment: More institutions and corporations might enter the crypto space,

potentially meaning broader acceptance and more legitimacy.

2. Better Regulations: If governments and regulating authorities can finally show up with better-framed regulatory frameworks, it will instill more confidence among people and business adoption.

3. Technological Advances: Steps in blockchain technology, such as scalability and security, might extend the use of cryptocurrencies in everyday life.

4. Financial Inclusion: Virtual currencies like these can definitely aid in the facilitation of financial services among the unbanked and underbanked sections of society and hence are likely to be extremely popular in developing regions.

5. Integration with Traditional Finance: The more different sorts of platforms and services are integrated with traditional financial systems, the easier it becomes to deal in or invest in digital assets.

6. CBDCs: Equally plausible, CBDCs presently under consideration, in other jurisdictions, may have a spillover impact on the wider diffusion of digital currencies generally.

While promising, a number of issues related to security, regulatory compliance, and market volatility have to be faced if wider diffusion is to be considered.

58..Which countries are crypto friendly today:

The following are the countries which have been considered to be crypto-friendly, having supportive regulatory environments and adopting cryptocurrency technologies. They would include:

1. Switzerland: It keeps some of the friendliest regulations in the world concerning cryptocurrencies, at the same time harboring innovation hubs like "Crypto Valley."

2. Singapore: It has a rather lucid regulatory environment, and it has grown really into one of the major epicenters in the world for cryptocurrency and blockchain.

3. Estonia: It also supports crypto startups and has been so friendly in implementing lenient regulations concerning blockchain technology.

4. Malta: It is positioning itself as a "Blockchain Island" by having very friendly, regulating conditions with respect to crypto-currencies and blockchain businesses.

5. Portugal: It assumes such friendly treatment with respect to taxes, without charging any form of capital gains tax for crypto investment in the case of individuals.

6. Germany treats Bitcoin as a legal means of payment and gives quite clear laws respecting crypto taxation and regulation.

It is, therefore, actually very conducive to innovation and investment, given that these countries have been very proactive in either the field of cryptocurrency or blockchain technology.

59..Biggest owners of Bitcoin today:

These days, the largest Bitcoin owners range from early adopters to huge institutional investors, to companies dealing in Bitcoin. A look at some of the largest holders.

1. Satoshi Nakamoto: - Estimated Holdings: 1 million BTC (approximately $60 billion at the price of a BTC of $60,000) It is assumed that Satoshi Nakamoto, the pseudonymous founder of Bitcoin, mined around 1 million BTC in the early ages of Bitcoin and never moved his wallet yet; thus, he is considered the biggest single holder of Bitcoin.

2. Public Companies: - MicroStrategy: Holdings: More than 152,000 BTC - over $7.5 bln when one BTC trades at $60,000. MicroStrategy is an enterprise analytics and business intelligence software company headquartered in Virginia. It is currently the largest public company holding Bitcoin, while its CEO is Michael Saylor. It started its aggressive accumulation of Bitcoin toward the end of 2020 as part of its treasury strategy. - Tesla: - Holdings: Roughly 10,725 BTC (more than $643 million at a BTC price of $60,000). Tesla, the electric carmaker headed by Elon Musk, invested in Bitcoin among its investment plans at the start of 2021. Tesla's Bitcoin investment fluctuates in value after some sales and changes in the market. - Marathon Digital Holdings: Holdings: around 12,964 BTC (valued at over $777 million at a BTC price of $60,000) - MDH stands for Marathon Digital Holdings, officially, is a cryptocurrency mining company holding a significant amount of mined Bitcoin from its operations.

3. Investment Funds in Bitcoins: - Gray Scale Investment Trust's Bitcoin Investment Trust (GBTC), Holdings: More than 600,000 BTC-valued at close to $36 billion if the price of one BTC is at $60,000. - Grayscale Bitcoin Trust is the largest Bitcoin investment vehicle that gives institutional and accredited investors a chance to take a position in Bitcoin exposure without holding the asset. It's a single holder of some of the largest amounts of Bitcoin. - Block.one: - Holdings: close to 140,000 BTC, worth more than 8.4 billion dollars when one BTC is traded for 60,000 dollars. -Block.one, the company behind the creation of the EOS blockchain, reportedly kept a pretty large amount of Bitcoin in its treasury.

4. Exchanges: - Binance: Holdings: This is considered to be among the largest digital assets exchanges; hence, it has a very high value of Bitcoin stored in wallet deposits and provided for liquidity in trading. Holdings are private but estimated by the amount of Bitcoin stored. - Coinbase: Holdings: A good number of BTCs are held in hot wallets, like Binance, on behalf of all its customers, since it is one of the biggest Exchanges in the United States and globally.

5. Other major holders: - The Winklevoss Twins - Holdings: Estimated to own somewhere in the region of 70,000 BTC - at an approximate value of over $4.2 billion at a BTC price of $60,000. Binance chief executive Changpeng Zhao - better known as CZ - is among the richest people in cryptocurrency, along with Cameron and Tyler Winklevoss, founders of the Gemini cryptocurrency exchange. They were among the earliest investors in Bitcoin and can still boast of being two of the largest holders of the cryptocurrency.

- Private Whales: There is a good number of private ownerships of Bitcoin, normally referred to as whales. They might be early adopters or technology entrepreneurs and anonymous investors. Sometimes, the exact identity of this kind of investor is not known, neither how many of the currencies they hold.

Conclusion: The most famous big owners nowadays include early adopters such as Satoshi Nakamoto, huge public companies like MicroStrategy and Tesla, the biggest investment funds like Greyscale, exchanges, and big private people so-called whales. Aggregated, this type of holder possesses an appreciable percentage of the total supply of Bitcoin and, therefore, contributes to driving the market dynamics.